Making a Laminated HollowBody Electric Guitar

by

Jim English

authorHOUSE

1663 LIBERTY DRIVE, SUITE 200
BLOOMINGTON, INDIANA 47403
(800) 839-8640
www.authorhouse.com

© 2005 Jim English
All Rights Reserved.

No part of this book may be reproduced, stored in a retrieval system, or transmitted by any means without the written permission of the author.

First published by AuthorHouse 02/23/05

ISBN. 1-4184-6065-6 (e)
ISBN: 1-4184-5135-5 (sc)

Library of Congress Control Number: 2003099363

This book is printed on acid-free paper.

Printed in the United States of America
Bloomington, Indiana

Text photos by Jim English
Front cover photo of Jim by Nancy Robbins Photography
Guitar Model Photos and Cover Design by Richard Glick of Fine Guitar Consultants and Jim English

ABOUT THE AUTHOR

The author has been playing guitar for 55 years and making them for 10 years. With the encouragement of people like Chet Atkins and Bob Benedetto, he decided to write a book on how to make laminated guitars. It is the only book on this type of construction and took four years to complete.

Jim can be reached at:
    Jim English
    14586 Olive Vista Dr.
    Jamul, CA 91935
    Check out his website at:
    englishguitars.com

DEDICATION

To Toni, my wife – Angela, my daughter and Jay, my son.

Jim English

April, 2002

ACKNOWLEDGEMENTS

This is probably the hardest part of writing this book, because I have so many people to thank that I hardly know where to begin. Truth be known, none of us got where we are without a lot of help from a lot of people.

A special thanks to Chet Atkins for his suggestions and encouragement through the years. His forty plus years of influence on me has dictated the sound that I love and the style that I play. He is a true genius and a nicer person you will never meet.

The most important thing for me to acknowledge is the fact that I am not a writer. I have tried to present information on a subject so vast that even attempting to do so is an exercise in futility. Still, I found such a need for doing it that I felt I must make the attempt. Most everyone that I have spoken with on the subject of making a laminated arch top guitar left me with the definite impression of regret for the fact that information about it was virtually non-existent. These people are suppliers, builders, businesses, musicians, repairmen, and authors. I'm only hoping this small work will be seen as an acceptable beginning by my peers.

To my friend and fellow luthier, David Johnson, of Campton, N.H., my special thanks for starting me on this new and exciting adventure.

Without my first two guitars being paid for in advance by my friends Jim Nelson and George Alexander, I would not have been able to consider this present work.

Don MacRostie and Dan Erlewine of Stewart McDonald's and Hideo Kamimoto of Kamimoto Guitars of San Jose, California spent lots of time on the phone with me openly sharing their knowledge and giving me encouragement. I am utilizing Mr. Kamimoto's truss rod curve design on my guitars.

Dave Vinopal and the membership of ASIA, through their publications, have been a source of information and inspiration. My thanks to all of them.

Mike Allen, who has passed away, also helped to influence the sound that I want to produce.

My mother, Linda English, encouraged my musical endeavors and never failed to be supportive in anything that I attempted.

Bob Benedetto, of Benedetto Guitars, in Florida, arguably, the worlds' finest arch top guitar maker, has graciously contributed the foreword to this book. He has unselfishly given of his time and knowledge. Stumped many times, it took only a phone call to him to solve my problem and receive encouragement. He is the person who convinced me to write this book. I am deeply indebted to him, and am proud and privileged to call him friend.

To my family, especially to my wife Toni who has never discouraged me from trying anything. Her infinite patience with my spending habits and projects is legendary.

To Richard Glick of Fine Guitar Consultants for the photo work on the cover and my different models at the back section of the book.

And finally to Jeremy Clifton for producing the illustrations on his computer and to Kristin Hargrove for converting all my hen scratchings to readable print.

TABLE OF CONTENTS

DEDICATION vii

ACKNOWLEDGEMENTS ix

FOREWORD BY BOB BENEDETTO xiii

AN AFTER WORD xv

PREFACE xvii

LIST OF FIGURES xxi

LIST OF PHOTOS xxv

INTRODUCTION xxvii

CHAPTER 1 1
    WORK AREA, GAINING BACKGROUND

CHAPTER 2 3
    THIS MATTER OF WOOD

CHAPTER 3 7
    MAKING THE TOP AND BACK

CHAPTER 4 13
    MAKING THE SIDES AND BUILDING THE BODY

CHAPTER 5 31
    INSTALLING THE HEADBLOCK, TAILBLOCK, NELSON TONE BAR
    STABILZER AND KERFING

CHAPTER 6 43
    INSTALLING THE BACK, STRAPBLOCK, PICKGUARD BRACKET BLOCK,
    JACK HOLE, NEC - LOC PIN, SPRAY LACQUER, LABEL

CHAPTER 7 51
    MAKING THE NECK

CHAPTER 8 63
    MAKING AND INSTALLING THE TRUSS ROD

CHAPTER 9 73
    FRETBOARDS

CHAPTER 10 ....**79**
    INSTALLING THE HEADSTOCK VENEER, FRETBOARD AND FRETS

CHAPTER 11 ....**93**
    THE NECK – FINAL SHAPING

CHAPTER 12 ....**99**
    FITTING THE TOP, CUTTING AND BINDING 'F' HOLES, INSTALLING BRACING

CHAPTER 13 ....**113**
    INSTALLING THE TOP, CUTTING THE PICKUP HOLES, BINDING THE BODY

CHAPTER 14 ....**117**
    DRILLING TUNER HOLES IN HEADSTOCK, FINISHING THE FRETS, INSTALLIING THE NECK TO THE BODY

CHAPTER 15 ....**125**
    APPLYING THE FINISH

CHAPTER 16 ....**135**
    FINAL ASSEMBLY
    INSTALL ELECTRONICS, TUNERS, TRUSS ROD COVER, TAILPIECE, STRAP BUTTONS, PICKGUARD, NUT, BRIDGE

CHAPTER 17 ....**145**
    SET UP

APPENDIX **157**

DESCRIPTION OF ENGLISH GUITARS MODELS..**173**

FOREWORD BY BOB BENEDETTO

About a year ago, I'd had several conversations with Jim English over archtop guitarmaking techniques. Jim had my book, *Making an Archtop Guitar,* and we were discussing methods relating to laminated body construction. He was actively making a full line of these popular archtops with his work well-received. After one such phone call, impressed by his enthusiasm and focus, I told him, "Jim, you should write your *own* book!" So, here it is!

The hollow body electric has been played in every possible venue and appreciated by both players and listeners for decades. Laminated tops and backs are stronger and less temperamental than their carved cousins, making the hollow bodied archtop a practical and dependable instrument. A true workhorse guitar, its versatility is unrivaled.

With unbridled determination, Jim has taught himself all there is to know about the construction of this popular instrument. The following pages are riddled with photos and precise drawings which depict his methodical approach to making the laminated archtop. He gives concise instructions widely accepted within the manufacturing industry, coupled with his own creative construction techniques. His book encompasses every aspect, from wood selection to set-up. The result is a straightforward book written so anyone can understand it and make a wonderful musical instrument for themselves or others to enjoy.

When a person with a passion for anything decides to share his knowledge, he deserves an audience. Jim's book will definitely draw a crowd.

ROBERT BENEDETTO
April 1998

Drawing by
Cindy Benedetto

AN AFTER WORD

When I was a young teenager, I played Chet Atkins style on my "other orange guitar." It's neck was unstable, it played almost in tune, and generally was what most of us "orange guitar lovers" had to put up with.

Fast forward to 1998, when I first discovered the gifted Jim English and his ability to address the issue of getting "that orange sound" into a proper instrument. Jim English Is one of the more focused individuals I have ever met. He has listened to nothing but Chet Atkins' music since he was a boy. He Is a dedicated player of that style, as well as an enthusiastic advocate of a contagious new thumbstyle that players want to learn as soon as they are exposed to it.

A celebrated knife designer and maker, Jim is used to working to exacting specifications, getting everything to fit…just right. His guitars sound so lush and play so well that when playing "'in the zone," the instrument disappears in the players hands. That is the goal, after all.

I am proud to represent Jim English, as he stands shoulder to shoulder with some of the finest makers of hand made guitars at Fine Guitar Consultants, San Diego, California. Every client that we have arranged a custom English guitar for has been pleased beyond their expectation.

As you read this book, you will learn well from an authority on the subject of the laminated guitar. Jim's work speaks volumes.

Richard Glick
fineguitanconsultants.com
April 2002

PREFACE

THE PURPOSE OF THIS BOOK

It is not the purpose of this book to present the history or origins of music as it relates to guitars. There are many excellent books that do not need to be "extended" shall we say. The electric guitar was basically invented in the USA. People like Paul Bigsby, Leo Fender, Chet Atkins, Merle Travis and Les Paul had a hand in the design and further evolution of what there is in the guitar world today for all of us to enjoy.

It is also not the purpose of this book to imply that my method of building is the only one that you should use. To my knowledge, however, there is only one small work available on the construction of laminated guitars. This is in spite of the fact that during the 50's and 60's and beyond, literally thousands of guitars were made that way. These guitars and the sounds they produced are enjoying a comeback - especially the Nashville sound of the early Gretschs and Gibsons - and the prices of these vintage instruments have skyrocketed out of the reach of the average person.

This book is not intended to be the bible of guitar making but rather a guide in making a particular type of guitar and a stepping stone to further study in the field of Lutherie. To try to include all the information available on guitar making and background would not only be presumptuous on my part but also require many volumes. Several large and well-written books are already available. They are excellent works indeed, but leave dozens of questions unanswered. Study and experience are necessary to complete the journey, probably only to discover how much is not known, but still to be learned.

This book is meant to enable someone with modest means to put together an excellent guitar - one very similar to those that were produced during the "Golden Age" of guitars. At that point the student may have some ideas or changes that he or she would like to incorporate into their next effort. Guitars over the next twenty years could evolve into something quite different and better than the present day. Hopefully, I may help that change come about through the writing of this book.

During the research for and the making of my guitars, I discovered a lot of misinformation. Techniques may vary. Tools may vary. Different methods might be used to arrive at the same result. But there are some things that should not be done if you are to make a good instrument.. I will try to point these out as we proceed through the process.

Again, you must bear in mind that we are not making a carved arch top guitar but a laminated one. This changes the rules somewhat concerning wood and techniques. Wood is very critical to the carved arch top as the finished sound depends almost entirely on the processing of the wood, adequate air chamber size, F hole (or round hole) dimension and bracing placement, etc. These factors will not be so critical to us as 70-80% of the sound will be generated from the type and placement of the pickups and their companion electronics. Only 20-30% of the sound will come from the guitar itself. This affords us more latitude in construction techniques. In my opinion, one is no better than the other, it's a difference in what you like or want.

If you wish to make a carved arch top type guitar, then this book may help in rounding out your knowledge. Bob Benedetto's book and video are the finest of their kind for that. They are also the only existing works on the subject. I believe that the type of guitar covered in this book will probably appeal to a larger cross section of people because of cost, versatility and ease of making by comparison. The laminated type can be made more beautiful, as far as looks are concerned, because you are not limited to the type of wood used for the top of the guitar. The many different beautiful veneers that are available make this possible. Veneers also add strength, and can produce a sound all their own.

I use some pre-made parts like kerfing and slotted fretboards. As you become more advanced and financially able, you may want to procure your own supply of ebony and produce the fretboards. It is very expensive and hard work, requiring the necessity to store, dry, and process your own. Not to mention precision slotting for accurate fretting. The theory of even-tempered scale tuning and fretboard slotting is long and complicated. Several books have been written on the subject. A particularly good one is by Hideo Kamimoto.

I also made my own body molds as I had no information at the time that would help me. I looked at vacuum presses, hydraulic presses, etc. and arrived at what seemed the surest way of succeeding. The technique worked very well and I will cover it later along with information on alternate methods. This format of alternate methods will be followed throughout the book so as to make more choices available. That way you are free to experiment with different methods, and arrive at one that may suit your needs better.

Most importantly - this is probably the first guitar that you have tried to make. View it as a learning experience. Do not rush. Try to do the best you can at each step of the process. The whole project will be that much more enjoyable and you will very likely produce an excellent instrument as well.

Before beginning, try to familiarize yourself with things such as tuners, bridges, tailpieces, pickguards - you know, the guitar trimmings. That way you will be able to decide up front what you want to use on your guitar. These decisions may change your process along the way and it is important to decide these things beforehand.

LIST OF FIGURES

1. Quartersawn End Grains
2. Flatsawn End Grains
3. Spacers Around Mold
4. Mold Alignment Marks
5. Mold Tracing
6. & 7 Making Mold
8. Drawing Trim Line
9. Cutting Mold
10. Finished Mold
10a. Notch at Top
11. Plexiglass Template
12. Cutting Template
13. Making Side Presses
14. Female Side of Mold
15. Flats for Clamping
16. Flat for Clamping Headblock
17. Headblock
18. Tailblock
19. Headblock Dimensions
20. Tailblock Fit
21. Everything in Position
22. Tone Bar
23. Drill Nec-Loc Pin Hole
24. Strap Block Location
25. Pickguard Block Location
26. Jack Hole Location
27. Label Location
28. Two Flatsawn Boards On Edge
29. Neck Pattern
30. Marking Neck Pattern On Board

31. Cut End At 4° Angle
32. Cutting Tenon On Neck
33. Cutting 15° Angle On Neck
34. Headstock Joint Orientation
35. Aligning Headstock
36. Cut and Sand Headstock
37. Cutting Rabbit On Neck End
38. Truss Rod Slot
38a. Bending Truss Rod
39. Anchor Hole for Truss Rod
40. Marking Between 4th and 5th Fret
41. Truss Rod Specs
42. Drilling 0.375 Stock
43. Bend and Thread .188 Truss Rod
44. & 45. Cutting Fretboard Ends
46. Shaping Fretboard
47. Fret Slots To Correct Depth
48. Installing Black/White Binding
49. Continuing Centerline On Fretboard Extension Piece
50. Cutting Headstock Veneer
51. Veneer Location
52. Cutting Headstock Binding Grooves
53. Binding Groove Dimensions
54.& 55. Glueing On Fretboard and Binding
56. File Binding
57.& 58. Installing Headblock Binding
59. Binding Location
60. Fretwire Configuration
61. Fretwire and Trimming
62. Fret Markers
63. Drawing In Neck Thickness
64. Thick Area at Head End

65. Neck Contour Shapes
65a. 'F' Hole Pattern
66. 'F' Hole Location
67. Mitre 'F' Hole Binding
68. Bracing Locations
69. Locating Pick-Ups
70. Braces Perpendicular
71. Shaping Braces
72. Glueing Top On
73. Body Binding Specs
74. Pre-Glueing Purfling
75. Mitre Binding On Back
76. Bottom Seam On Binding
77. Tuner Locations
78. Fret Dressing
79. Nec-Loc Notch
80. Everything On Centerline
81. Straight Edge On Frets
82. Electronics Schematics
83. Truss Rod Cover
84. Pickguard
85. Bridge Base
86. Radius On Bridge Base
87. Nut and Bridge Shaping
88. Slanting String Slots
89. Installing Strings On Posts
90. Radius at Fretboard and Bridge
91. Plucked String Path
92. Neck Bow Under Tension

LIST OF PHOTOS

1. Cutting 1" Out of Plaster of Paris Mold
2. Using Ford Van as Press
3. Gretsch Guitar as Model for Mold
4. Making Side Presses
5. Initial Cutting of Side Presses
6. Finished Side Presses
7. Electric Bending Iron
7a. Propane Bending Iron
8. Lined Mold with Center Line Marked
9. Glass Flat Sanding Surface
10. &10a. Outer Veneer Glued to One Half of Body
11. Marking Sides for Trimming
12. Marked Centerline On Inner Veneer
13. Glueing Up In Press
13a. Body Mold
14, 14a Kerfing Glued In
14b. Sides In Mold with Head and Tailblock and Nelson Tone Bar
15. Back Clamped
16. Strap Block Installed
17. Pickguard Block Installed
18. Making Side Cuts On Table Saw
18a. Finished Cuts
19. Making Vertical Cuts
19a. Finished Tenon
20. Glueing Headstock to Neck
21. & 21a. Truss Rod Slot Cutting Jig
22., 22a., & 22b. Router Set-Up
23. Cutting Truss Rod Nut Slot in Headstock
24. Clamping Truss Rod Slot Filler
25. Headstock Logo Inlay

26. Glueing Headstock Veneer
27. Glueing Headstock Binding
28. Installing Frets
29. Shaping and Sanding Neck
30. 'F' Hole Cutting Jig
30a., 30b., & 30c. Pin Router
31. Scribing the Top Braces
31a. Clamping and Glueing Braces
31b. Braces Finished
32. Trimming Fret Ends
32a. Dressing Fret Tops
33. Marking Neck Extension
33a. Trimming Neck Extension
34. Glueing Neck On
35. Guitar Masked Off
36. Stain and Initial Coats of Finish Applied
37. Wet Sanding
38. Buffer
39. Bigsby Tailpiece
40. & 40a. Strap Buttons Installed
41. Studs Installed In Bridge Base
42. Marking Bridge for Trimming
43. Sanding Bridge Base

INTRODUCTION

MAKING A LAMINATED HOLLOW BODY ELECTRIC GUITAR

Dave Johnson once said to me, "Why don't you build one like that?" My answer to him was "Are you crazy? It takes a company full of magicians to do that!" Well, that wasn't true at all, as I was to learn.

My friend and I were talking in the shop one day several years ago, discussing his attempt to make a twelve string acoustic guitar. I had no doubt that he could do it and I was trying my best to encourage him. He is somewhat of a magician himself, being one of the best knife makers that I have ever met. I was fortunate enough to have him teach me what he knew of knife making, and now I was to come under his tutelage and influence in the field of lutherie. The very word conjures up an air of mystery! Webster says of it "one who makes stringed musical instruments". Boy, what an understatement! There is so much more involved!

I have always, it seems, used a variety of tools, both hand and power. Early on, I had used files, hammers, saws, drills, etc. I was always building something, even bird and doghouses. When I worked in aircraft, as I got better jobs in assembly and inspection, I learned to use precision tools such as calipers, micrometers, height gauges, and surface plates. On into knife making, I began to use grinders, drill presses and a whole new variety of tools and machinery. All during that time, I used a variety of materials - bone, steel, wood, ivory, micarta, mother of pearl and many others.

What I'm trying to say here is that when I decided to make a guitar it wasn't as if I was going to do something completely alien. The guitar was, yes, but the materials and tools weren't. The guitar, as an instrument, was not entirely new either, as I have been around the guitar since I was born. I have been playing since I was twelve or so. It may not be totally necessary to have a working background in tools and materials, but you can learn so much faster and do so much better at making your first few guitars if you have some experience with both.

Having decided to make a guitar, I had to decide just what kind to make. There are so many different kinds of guitars out there - Spanish, classical, nylon string, western steel string, flat tops, arch tops, and so on. I began playing along with Smokey's Valley Music Store on TV in the 50's. I heard Merle Travis and thought it was wonderful. Just as I had learned my first Travis tune, Fuller Blues, I heard a guy named Chet Atkins and knew I had found Heaven on Earth. About this time I saw Jimmy Webster demonstrate his touch technique on a Gretsch White Falcon and thought that it was the most beautiful guitar I had ever seen. Then, in 1956 I saw an orange Chet Atkins model 6120 Gretsch and bought it. I still have it. It is as beautiful now as it was then.

I discovered that Gretsch is no longer made in the US. I went to several music stores. Nobody had one. Not even close. Since that is the kind of guitar that I played and loved I decided to make a similar kind.

What I went through for eighteen months searching for materials, buying books, videos, gathering tools and knowledge and dealing with the many different aspects of the project would fill several books. What I have learned cannot be measured by any means that I know of. I have learned much and made many new friends. Separating the hype and other bad and useless information, I learned on my own. Searching for books and information on how to make a laminated guitar, I found that nothing was available in print, film, pictures or anything else. I discovered that getting certain information is like pulling hens' teeth. Some of that is tradition, some of it is trade secrets, and some of it is just plain selfishness and fear. But I have learned, in spite of that. Hoping to pass this knowledge on is part of the reason I have undertaken the task of writing this book. So join me now on a most incredible journey.

CHAPTER 1

WORK AREA, GAINING BACKGROUND

Many people begin a project without having an adequate work area. It is probably possible to make a guitar using nothing more than a kitchen table and a toolbox to house the equipment, but I wouldn't recommend it! Part of a garage is fine, if available, but remember you are working with wood and you need to control the humidity factor. You also need work benches and lots of drawer space for tools. They will stay much cleaner that way. Buy a good shop vacuum. Sears makes a good one for the price. Keep things clean and picked up. Lighting is a very important consideration. Good fluorescent lighting is worth its weight in gold. Since you will, at times, work in a dust filled atmosphere, a respirator mask and safety glasses are a must. You must also consider grounding all power equipment like grinders, buffers, etc. You might want to consider a large vacuum system with scoops under sanders, buffers and grinders. If you have the room you might want to consider building a spray booth and provide a storage area for finishing materials like lacquers. Be sure to provide adequate ventilation. Place mats on the floors to help when you will be standing for long period of time. Get the kind with holes as they help in catching debris and small parts that you might drop. If you will be using power sanders, grinders, and buffers, don't work in loose clothing as they can become caught and cause injury. Wear good shoes, possibly safety toe type as bruised or broken toes are not fun. A small radio playing your favorite music during quiet times is helpful. In general, be safe, have an adequate work area and good tools. You will find it more fun and you will do a much better job. Read through this book before you begin in order to familiarize yourself with the necessary tools and methods.

A very important part of making a guitar, or anything for that matter, is gathering information. Check out the supply list in the appendix. Buy some of the excellent books that are available on every phase of guitarmaking, like finishing, electronics, wood, etc. Many videos are also available. Go to music stores, talk to people, talk to other guitarmakers, and look at everything. Go to the library. It also helps to have access to several different types of guitars that you can look at and refer to. You would be surprised at how much you can learn just by looking! If your memory suffers, take notes. In other words, do your homework ahead of time. Learn all you can before you start. Jot down ideas, gather tools, etc. All of this will help you make the final decision that, yes, this is something you really want to do. Once you decide to do it, do all you can to prepare yourself. Enrolling in a woodshop class at college or continuation school or vocational school will really help. Realize also that it will require an outlay of a substantial amount of money, unless you already have the necessary space and tools for such an undertaking.

But most of all, TIME, will be the one factor that will place limitations on what you will or will not be able to accomplish. If you are married, your wife and family must be very understanding of the time that you take in being away from them. Your friends may not understand this sudden urge and commitment. Your job may not allow you all the time you need and you may find yourself robbing time from your weekends when you might otherwise be doing things with your family. Once you get started, you will meet a new companion named Murphy. He has a law that seems to work most of the time, if you let it. Get use to hauling Murphy around. Get good control of your emotions. In the next couple of years you may become so well acquainted with him that you will have to provide a space for him in your shop! All kidding aside, unless you proceed slowly, use good sense and remain calm, Murphy is perfectly capable of taking over and running things! Think things out beforehand, follow the sequences carefully and when mistakes happen, hold on to your temper and frustration. Don't be afraid or ashamed to ask for advice from experts. Back up and do more research until you find answers. Only then will you meet with success.

Well forewarned is forearmed, so let's get on with it!

CHAPTER 2

THIS MATTER OF WOOD

I write about wood first because it is the first consideration in making a guitar. When making a laminated hollow body electric guitar, the selection of wood is a different matter than when you are making a carved acoustic type. In the latter case many things such as tap tones, moisture content, etc. have to be considered.

In our case, we are using veneers, which, by the nature of their construction are very strong for a given thickness, and they are very stable. Shrinking and cracking are not a problem by comparison, provided you use a good quality wood (mahogany or poplar sandwiched with maple). You can also use all maple which gives a sharper sound - not so mellow. This is true of the top, back and sides. It is not true of the neck, head, neckblock, tailblock and bracing. These must be quartersawn as close to perfect as possible, and properly dried. Quartersawn wood is stronger and not as likely to warp or split. Quartersawn wood looks like Figure 1.

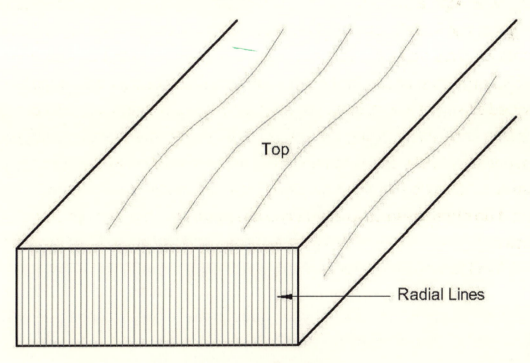

Figure 1 – Quartersawn End Grains

The grains are straight and close together and are perpendicular to the large face.

Flat sawn wood looks like Figure 2.

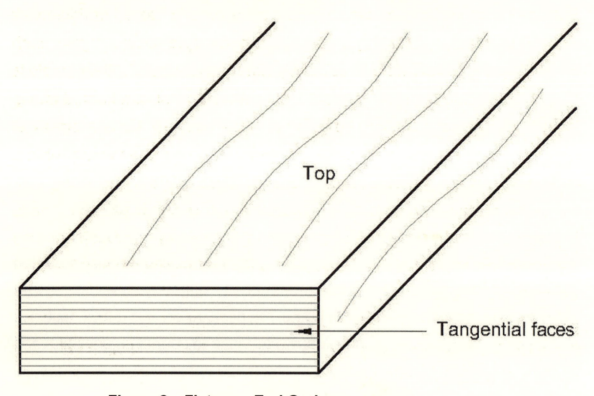

Figure 2 – Flatsawn End Grains

Figure 2 has tangential faces. This is very likely to warp and split.

Wood has certain moisture content. As it begins to lose this water, changes take place that result in warping, cracking, shrinking, etc. Evaporation or swelling (wood can gain as well as lose water because it is a hygroscopic material) occurs more on the tangential faces of wood than it does on the radial faces. (Fig. 1,2) The radial faces are, therefore, more stable and less likely to warp or twist, so that quartersawn wood is more dimensionally stable.

The matter of shop humidity is important, but not as critical as in carved construction. Somewhere in the range of 45 - 55% humidity is good. Remember that the winter months tend to be drier than the summer months, and some means must be employed to maintain evenness, such as a humidifier, etc. Store all of your wood in this environment if possible. A guitar made in a high humidity area will shrink and crack, if taken into a dry climate, as it loses moisture.

In the opposite case, wood can absorb more moisture without significant change (if it was made in low humidify conditions).

I don't care for the two-piece book matched top and back construction. The line down the middle, used to some advantage in flamed or fiddleback maple is somewhat distracting. One piece flamed maple veneer large enough for a 17" guitar is very hard to come by, but it can be found. Plain maple is easier to find and makes a great looking guitar. It's just that flamed maple is much more beautiful and appealing to many people. This is a matter of taste only (and higher cost), as the difference in sound is non-existent in a laminated guitar. Try to use eastern hard rock maple if possible.

The sides are to be laminated also. Here the inner veneers are made in two halves, then joined at the butt. A one-piece veneer is wrapped around the whole thing on the outside, eliminating the visible joint at the tail end of the guitar.

So, for the top and back, use one piece outer veneer whether it be flamed, quilted or plain. The outer veneer I use is .040 or .045 after thickness sanding. Two or three layers of thinner veneer make up the inner plies (with mahogany or poplar core) and add up to .060 or so for a total thickness of .120 - .130. This will give much better sound than if it is thicker. The order is maple, mahogany or poplar and the final outer veneer of .040 - .0450 maple for the top, back, and sides, although you can go to .150 - .160 thick for the sides. This will be covered more thoroughly when we get to the construction phase.

The wood for the neck and headstock is quartersawn and properly dried maple available from several different suppliers, listed in the appendix. The neckblock, tailblock, and bracing are also quartersawn. The neckblock and tailblock can be made from maple or mahogany. Although mahogany is lighter than maple, it would not look right as a neck on a maple guitar. Maple is very strong, doesn't move much under string tension, and matches the maple of the guitar, especially flamed or quilted. It is heavier but tends to balance on the guitars that I make. When you set the guitar on your knee, it should balance. Quartersawn kiln dried eastern hard rock maple makes an excellent neck and headstock material.

The fretboard material I use is ebony. Rosewood and maple are also used as fretboards. Rosewood tends to be somewhat porous and wears faster. I like ebony because it is very strong, stable, and hard and can be quite beautiful. Inlays show up very well on a black background. Gaboon ebony is the blackest available. I use it as my bridge base also. Be sure to buy from a reputable source. It must be quartersawn and properly dried. This is very hard to verify with ebony, hence the importance of a reliable source. Check the appendix.

Luthier Merchantile has a catalog which includes most of the information anyone would need concerning most of the woods needed for guitar construction.

This pretty much covers the basic woods on this type of guitar. More will be said as we progress.

Neck & Headstock Quartersawn Maple
Neck Block, Tailblock - Maple or Mahogany
Top & Back, .120 -.130
Sides - .150 -.160
Fretboard Ebony ① - Rosewood ②

CHAPTER 3

MAKING THE TOP AND BACK

Once you have done some background preparation and set up your shop, you are ready to begin.

Guitar making is made much simpler if you have a picture to refer to. Stewart McDonalds has a couple of different blueprints you can buy to familiarize yourself with dimensions, etc. I drew my own blueprint showing dimensions and I refer to it often. For that, go to a blueprint supply house and buy the supplies. Use the other drawings as examples.

I am going to tell you what I did and then you must decide how you want to do it. If you decide not to make your own molds, Stewart McDonalds offers pre-made arched laminated tops and backs. The drawback here is they have nothing but plain maple. The advantage of taking the time to make your own molds is that you can use outer veneers of your choice, once you can find them in one piece 18" x 22".

I was fortunate enough to have an older guitar with a good arch that I liked very much. I made a plaster of Paris mold of the back. My guitar was a single cutaway type. See Photo 3.

Photo 3 – Gretsch Guitar as Model for Mold

I made a piece that filled the cut-away so that when I made my mold, it could be used for a right or left hand guitar. Hold it in place with masking tape when making the mold. Line the surface of the guitar with waxed paper. Bend redwood garden molding on your bending iron (refer to Chapter 4 for information on bending irons) to match the shape of your guitar and tape it on creating a dam for the plaster of Paris. You can also use very thin wood or plastic garden edging material for this. Pour plaster of Paris at least 1½" thick. This step creates a negative mold. When you remove it, sand it very smooth inside. At this point, I cut 1" of length out of the middle of the mold and rejoined it with epoxy. See Photo 1.

Photo 1 – Cutting 1" Out of Plaster of Paris Mold

The reason for this is that my guitars are joined to the body at the 16th fret instead of the 14th fret. This would make the balance neck heavy as the guitar would be 1 1/8" longer overall. It would also not fit standard cases. The area from the back of the bridge to the tail end would also have increased by 1 1/8" making it look funny. Aesthetics are very important, as is balance.

Next create a dam around the outside of the mold adding ½" spacers of wood to make it slightly larger for trimming excess off the finished laminated top or back. Fill the gap with plaster of Paris and blend it in so it is flat. See Figure 3.

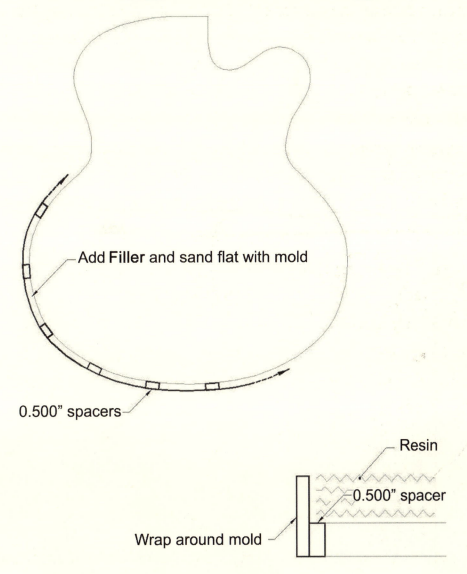

Figure 3 – Spacers Around Mold

Now pour in a strong two-part epoxy molding resin after spraying the surface with a release agent. When it is done, you have one half of your finished mold. Sand the surface until it is perfect. Next, put a dam around your finished epoxy mold, screw it to the sides, spray a release agent and pour

in the two-part resin. Now you have both halves of your mold. Before you separate them, make matching marks on all four sides so that later, you can line them up perfectly. See Figure 4.

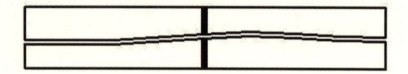

Figure 4 - Mold Alignment Marks

Now that your molds are ready, it's time to make your top and back. Of course by now you have decided on the overall shape and measurements of your guitar, such as upper and lower bout, waist and overall length, etc. Using your molds for size, trace your veneers and cut with a razor knife. See Figure 5.

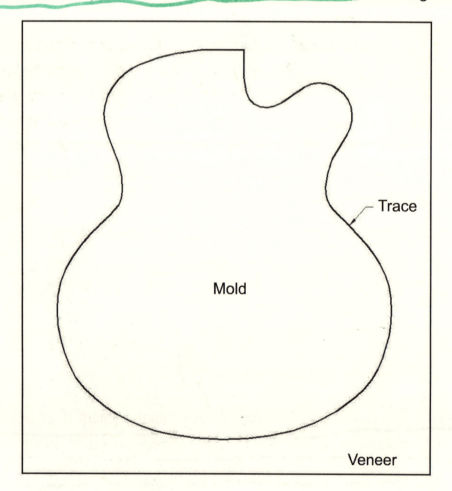

Figure 5 - Mold Tracing

10

TOP VENEERS

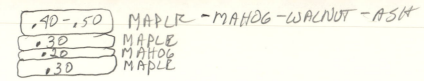

.40-.50) MAPLE - MAHOG - WALNUT - ASH
.30) MAPLE
.20) MAHOG
.30) MAPLE

Be careful as the end - grain at the edges tend to split easily on the veneers. My tops have an inner veneer of .030 maple, then .020 mahogany, then .030 maple and a final outer one piece veneer of .040 - .050 thickness for a finished thickness of .120 - .130. This is after thickness sanding of the outer veneer at a lumber supplier outlet. Be sure to sand the tight side only. Tight and loose sides refer to the tears and bumps that are present in maple veneers. The tight side has voids or tears that sand out beautifully whereas the loose side has bumps that when sanded off require too much filling and will leave holes in the final finish.

My outer veneers start at .060 and are sanded to .040 - .050. Curly maple veneer tends to tear easily so be careful. You can also use ash, walnut or oak for your final outer veneer. These will make some pretty guitars depending on the final finish used. Walnut can be light or dark stained and is quite beautiful. If you use mahogany as your outer veneers, this allows you to use mahogany for your neck and headstock.

Once your veneers are cut and ready, spread an aliphatic type glue (Franklin Titebond, not type II) evenly on both mating surfaces, but not super thick. Experience will tell you how much to use. Too much squeeze out is too much glue. No squeeze out is too little, etc. Place together between your molds and apply pressure. Since I did not have the finances to build a press, I looked around for an alternative method. I found it in the rear end of my Ford van. See Photo 2.

Photo 2 - Using Ford Van as Press

INSIDE - OUTSIDE MOLDS

As you let the weight down on the middle of your mold be sure that the alignment marks that you made earlier on the sides of your mold when they were perfectly aligned, line up once again during the pressing operation. Leave it for 6 - 8 hours if possible. This way the glue will dry hard, helping the top to hold its form better.

Actually, using a car for weight instead of a van should work also. I now use a 20 ton shop press, using my molds sandwiched between two 1" thick steel plates. The press is available from Harbor Freight Salvage Co. The cost is approximately $170.00.

Using the thicker veneer as an outer layer works very well. Turning the grain of the inner veneers in opposite directions from each other will make an even stronger top or back. When you sand the veneers during the finishing process, the thicker veneer allows for more sanding. Sanding too thin can cause bubbles when you apply the finish. This is critical when applying a water - based lacquer. They can have as much as 70% water and will soak through a thin veneer before they have flashed off enough to dry. The folks at FSM now make a water based lacquer that is only 5% water and it works great. It is available at Luthier Merchantile.

Set your top and back aside and we will come back to them later.

CHAPTER 4

MAKING THE SIDES AND BUILDING THE BODY

Before you can build the body and the sides, you must make a body mold and a set of side presses.

Begin your body mold by glueing three pieces of 3/4" plywood 22" x 24" together as in Figure 6. Draw a center line from end to end 24" long.

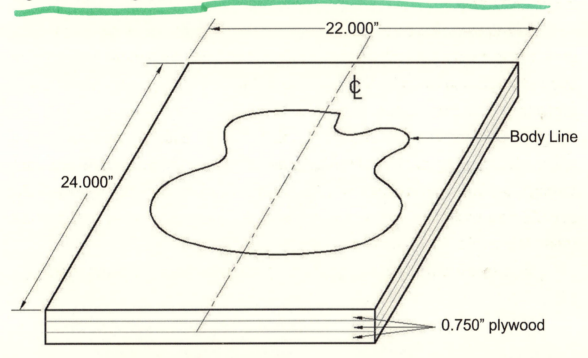

Figure 6 – Making Mold

Make a template of 1/4" or 3/8" plexiglass from your drawing to exact size. Mark exact center, lay it on your stack of plywood and mark it all the way around. See Figure 7.

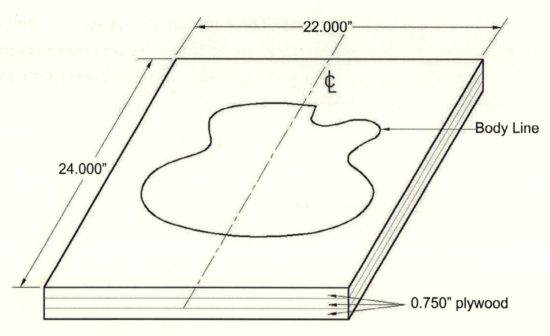

Figure 7 – Making Mold

Draw a line 2" away from the outline on the outside of the outline. See Figure 8.

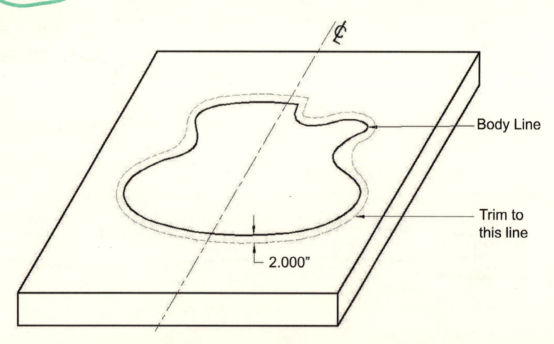

Figure 8 – Drawing Trim Line

Cut to this line on a bandsaw. Then cut down the center line, cutting the mold in half. Now trim exactly along the body line. Be very careful at the top. The lines A & B must be square to each other because this is where the headstock will be glued. See Figure 9.

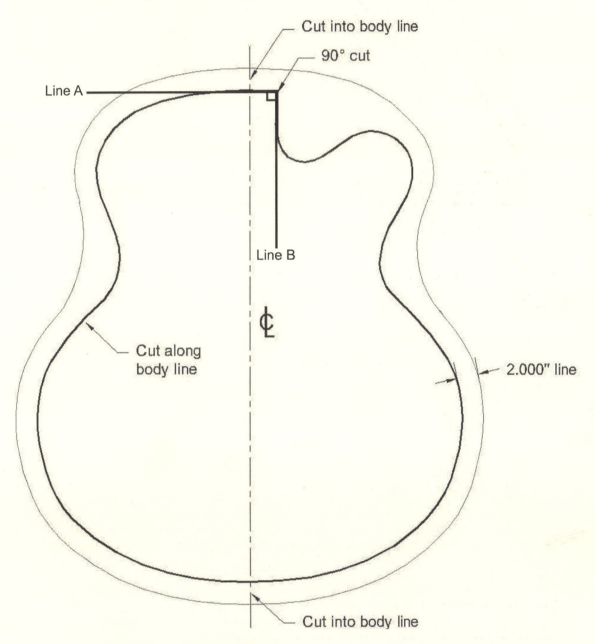

Figure 9 – Cutting Mold

When you are through cutting out the inside, clean up the sides by filing and or sanding, being sure that the sides are perpendicular to the top and bottom surfaces of the mold. Use glued in spacers at the top and bottom to achieve your exact measurements across the upper and lower bouts. Of course, you decided on the measurements when you made your drawing as to guitar size. My measurements are 12 1/4" upper bout and 17" lower bout. Your mold should look like this: See Fig. 10

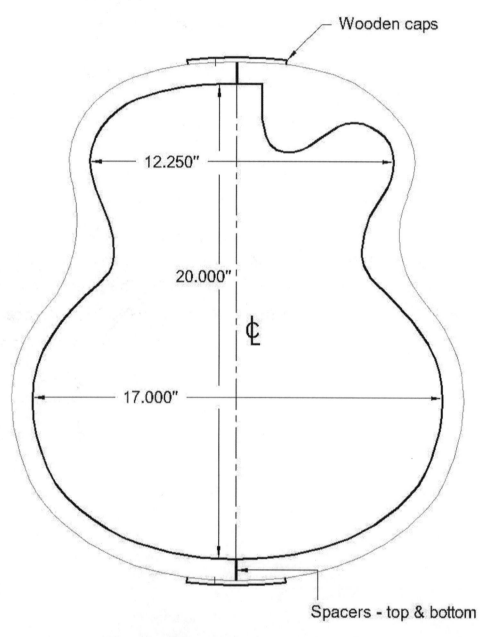

Figure 10 – Finished Mold

These are my dimensions. Of course, yours may vary. Mark the exact center line on the top and bottom. Now, at the top, make a notch 1/2" by 1/4". See Figure 10A.

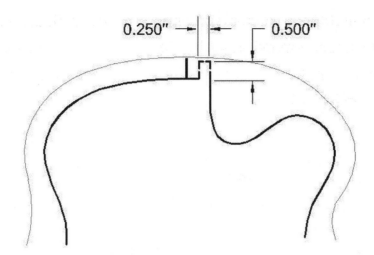

Figure 10a – Notch at Top

This will be explained later as we build the sides.

Smooth the inside surfaces of your mold and set it aside.

Before you can make the sides, you have to make a set of presses. These must be made as accurately as possible. The interior side of the presses must be without dips or they will show up on the finished sides. They must be made as strong as possible as you will be clamping them together, so I recommend using plywood.

Take the template you made of plexiglass and split it down the exact center. See Figure 11.

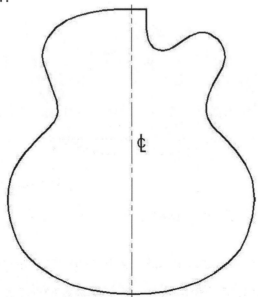

Figure 11 – Plexiglass Template

Now scribe a line around the outer edges (not along the center line) 1/2" in from the edge. See Figure 12.

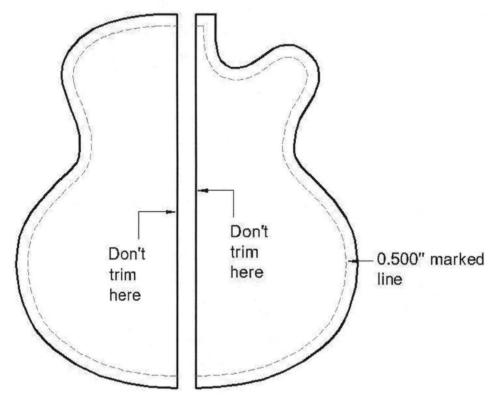

Figure 12 – Cutting Template

Trim to this line and smooth it perfectly. You now have two routing templates. Using 1/2" plywood, cut 14 pieces 22" x 24". This will make two equal stacks 3 1/2" high, made of 7 pieces each for a 3" thick guitar. This allows trimming the finished sides to be 2 3/4". The top and back make 1/4" total, giving the 3" measurement.

Using pieces of a 2 x 4, screw them down to your work bench, countersinking the screw heads. These are spacers under the plywood stack to allow for clearance of the router. Lay 1 sheet of plywood on top of the spacers and lay your template on top of it. Drill 3 or 4 holes through to your 2 x 4 spacers. Countersink the holes for the screw heads, and screw everything down tight. See Figure 13 and Photo 4.

Top View

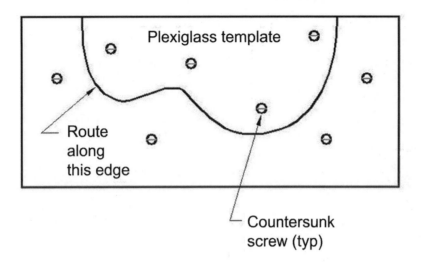

22.000" x 24.000"
0.500" plywood
screwed to spacers
on bench top

Side View

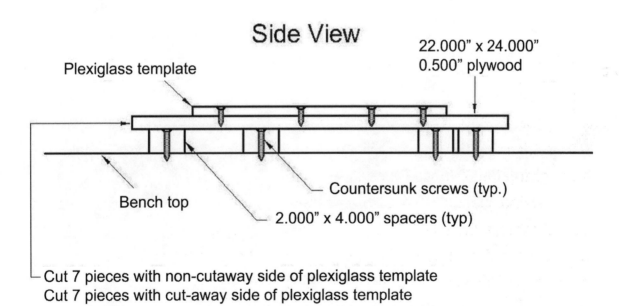

Cut 7 pieces with non-cutaway side of plexiglass template
Cut 7 pieces with cut-away side of plexiglass template

This makes a male and female side of the presses

Figure 13 – Making Side Presses

Photo 4 – Making Side Presses

Using a 1" diameter bearing and a 3/16" router bit, rout around the template on the curved side only. Be careful as both halves of the routed pieces will be used as a press. Do 7 pieces for each side this way. They should be all exactly the same and look like Figure 14 and Photo 5.

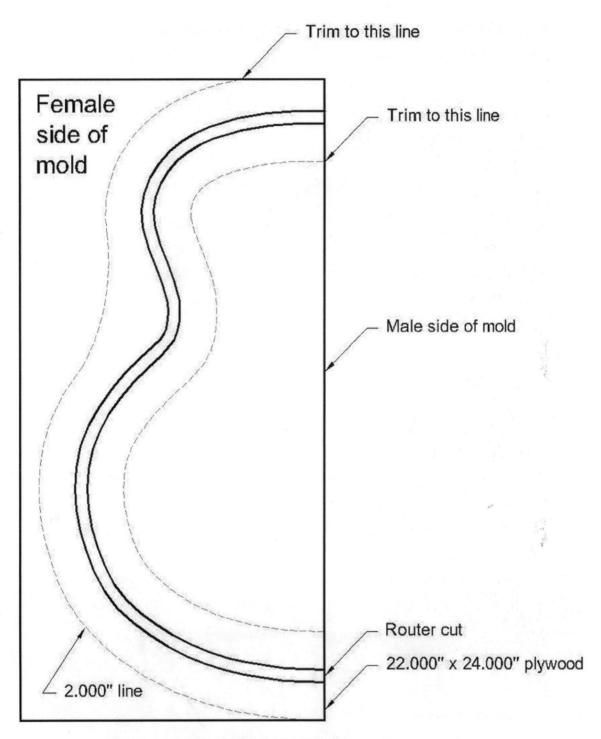

Figure 14 – Female Side of Mold

Photo 5 – Initial Cutting of Side Presses

You now have four stacks of 7 boards each. Glue the stacks together, using a square to align the curved surfaces exactly. Use long wood screws to cinch them down tight. Clean up the routed surfaces so that they are smooth and even with 200 grit paper. The surfaces must be square to the sides and very smooth, especially the female side of the mold. This will be the outside surface of the laminated sides. Now trim along the curved lines in 2" inches with a band saw. If you need to, a lumber yard will do this. You now have 4 pieces stacked 7 high, glued together. Refer to Figure 14 and Photo 6.

Photo 6 – Finished Side Presses

Make 5 or 6 flat areas to facilitate clamping. See Figure 15.

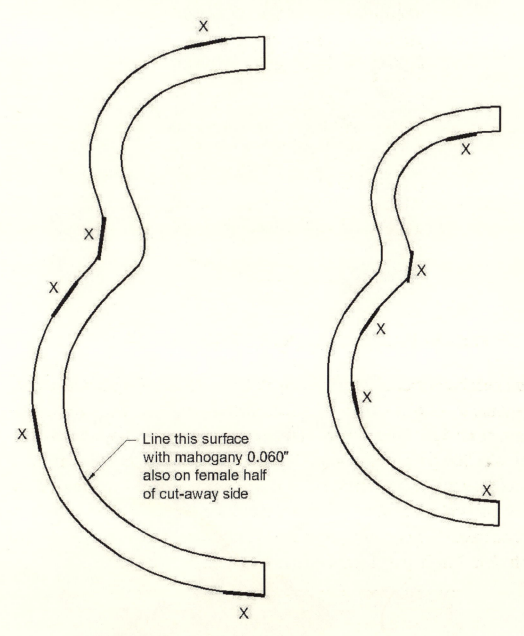

Line this surface with mahogany 0.060" also on female half of cut-away side

Figure 15 – Flats for Clamping

Buy an electric bending iron or make a bending iron of 2 1/2" diameter thick walled aluminum pipe 14" long. Clamp it in your vise and use a propane torch in the end to heat it. See Photo 7 & 7A.

Photo 7 – Electric Bending Iron

Photo 7a – Propane Bending Iron

Now, line the female halves on your presses with .060 mahogany veneer. Start with a 4" x 36" x .060 piece of mahogany. A piece of .040 will also work.

Pre-bend it to fit with your bending iron as follows: spray the area of the wood to be bent with a mist type sprayer using distilled water. The minerals in tap water will discolor the white maple wood you will be bending later when you make your sides. Experience will tell you how wet to get the wood and how hot to get your bending iron. Practice on scrap pieces. Move the wet wood back and forth while putting slight pressure in the direction you want to bend it. As the moisture in the wood heats up and vaporizes, it renders the wood soft and bendable. Hold it in that position until it cools and it will retain its shape. Other types and sizes of bending irons are available but a small propane heated one is adequate for our purposes since we will not be bending any wood over .060 thick. Bend slowly and in steps keeping the wood wet to prevent splitting, especially with curly maple. Also be sure to let it dry before trying to glue it. Now clamp the bent piece between the two halves of your press to be sure of a tight fit. Use shims on the male side if you have to for a tight fit. You are going to glue it to the female side. When the fit is right, apply glue and clamp together. Leave it for two hours. Remove the clamps, trim, sand and spray the surface with 2 - 3 coats of a good sanding sealer, making a very smooth, even surface on the female half of each press. Final sand to 400 grit. See Photo 8.

Photo 8 – Lined Mold with Center Line Marked

SIDES

INSIDE .030 MAPLE .040
MIDDLE .060 MAHOG .040
OUTSIDE .060 MAPLE .040

INSIDE MAPLE .080 - .090
OUTSIDE MAPLE .090 - .050

Mark the exact center lines at the bottom of both presses.

Once your presses are ready, it is time to make the sides. The space between your presses after using a 3/16" router bit and lining one side with .040 - .060 mahogany will be .125 -.135. This will be ±.010 - .015 because of the give in the wood when using strong clamps. I have varied it even more with no problem. Depending on the thickness of my veneers. I try to end up with .060 - .090 or so before the addition of the outer veneer. You can use .030 maple, .060 mahogany or maple with an outer wrap of .060 maple. You could also use all maple, but a core of mahogany or poplar gives a slightly warmer sound. If using all maple, a two piece of .060 inner and .060 outer wrap is good.

Cut your pieces 3 1/2" x 36". Bend to fit and pre-clamp to check fit. When the fit is good and tight, glue up and clamp. Franklin Tite Bond glue works very well for this. Spread the glue evenly using an old credit card. Put glue on each surface. Use waxed paper underneath to make clean-up easier. Leave clamped in the press for 11/2 hours. Then take it out and remove any excess glue from the surfaces of the sides and the press. Reclamp it in the press (you don't have to clamp it quite as hard this time) and leave it for at least 8 hours. This lets the glue set up hard and helps the sides retain their shape better. The sides should be nice and square without any marks or "valleys" on the outside. This is why you lined your pieces and sanded it so carefully – to eliminate any bumps or depressions from showing up on the finished surface.

One alternate method is to start with a single piece of maple thickness sanded to .080 - .090. Carefully bend it on your bending iron to fit your press precisely. I have not used this method, but several books have been written on how to do this as it is a more standard technique. If you choose to do it this way, it will work fine.

Either way, you end up with two sides to be joined at the butt end and wrapped with a single piece of .040 - .060 maple veneer, making very strong sides and eliminating the visible seam at the butt joint which is usually hidden with some sort of inlay. I believe this one piece outer wrap technique is stronger. Try to use an outer veneer that closely matches your top and back in color and pattern. This makes a nicer visual package upon completion.

When you remove your sides from the presses, sand the outer surface with a flat sanding block and 220 grit to remove any left over glue. Be careful not to sand too much. Removing .010 won't hurt much. Also clean up the inner face of glue, etc. Check the size by fitting to your mold. Make sure the edges have no hollow spots where there was no glue. Fill any holes with glue along the edges.

Make a flat sanding surface by placing a piece of 1/4" tempered glass 2' x 3' on a very flat surface. I use a piece of hollow core door. Using 3M Spray Adhesive, stick sheets of 100 grit sanding paper to the glass. See Photo 9.

Photo 9 – Glass Flat Sanding Surface

Now sand 1 edge of each side piece flat on your sanding surface. Using your mold as your guide, cut excess off the butt of both pieces so that when placed together the measurement across the lower bout is 17" or whatever size you have decided on for your guitar. Be sure the cut edges are squared to the sanded edge and fit together with no gap. Final fit with a file.

You are now ready to glue the one piece outer veneer in place. Cut the veneer 3 1/2" x 68". Using the bending iron, bend the cut-out side first for a perfect fit together. The glueing is done 1 side at a time in your glueing presses. Clamp up dry and while clamped, mark the inner piece just short of the center line (which is marked on the butt end of the female half of the press). See Photo 10, 10A & 12.

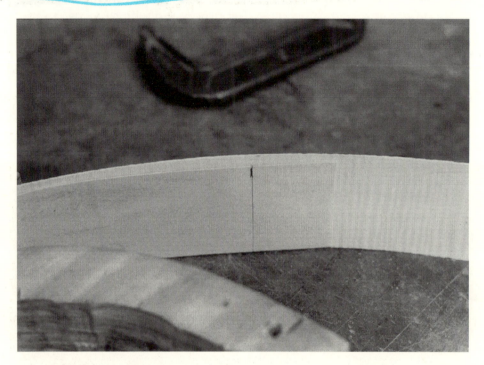

Photo 12 – Marked Centerline On Inner Veneer

Photo 10 & 10a – Outer Veneer Glued to One Half of Body

Trim square to this mark. When the fit is right, glue up the cut-out side first, putting glue on both surfaces and clamp for 1 1/2 hours. See Photo 13.

Photo 13a – Body Mold

Carefully remove from press, clean excess glue, especially from the joint area at the butt end. Replace in press and reclamp for 6 - 8 hours. Remove and clean up.

Now go to your mold and fit the glued up side in the mold. Clamp in place. Mark and bend the other side to fit exactly. Bend slowly to prevent flammed maple from splitting. Put inner veneer in place, trim at butt and make sure of an exact fit. Then, go back to the press, apply glue and glue that side up as before. See Photo 13 and 13A. Remove in 1½ hours, clean up and install in the mold. Clamp in place and let set 6 - 8 hours.

So, you used the press first for the cut-out side, then you use the mold to fit the other side, then glue up in the press. After that, clamp in mold. After 6 - 8 hrs. in mold, remove & mark one side with a surface gage & pencil evenly. See Photo 11. Trim to this line. Sand the surface on your flat plate. Turn over and mark the other surface a 2.750. Trim to this line and sand flat. When you add the top and back thicknesses to this (each .125) the finished thickness of your guitar will be 3.000".

Your rim assembly is now made and ready for the next step.

Photo 11 – Marking Sides for Trimming

CHAPTER 5

INSTALLING THE HEADBLOCK, TAILBLOCK, NELSON TONE BAR STABILZER AND KERFING

Place your glued up sides in the body mold. Trim the upper part of the cut-out side to fit in the notch of the mold. See Figure 16.

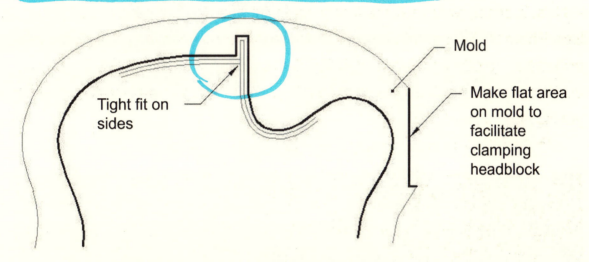

Figure 16 – Flat for Clamping Headblock

Working your way around from the cut-out, clamp the body into the mold and at the top of the non-cutaway side, trim to fit tight. Refer to Figure 16.

I use quartersawn mahogany for my head and tailblock and quartersawn maple for the tone bar. Spruce or bass wood can also be used for the head and tailblock. Cut a piece of mahogany or whatever material you have decided to use to the following dimensions: 2.750" high x 2.500" wide x 3.000" long and the end grains oriented as in Figure 17.

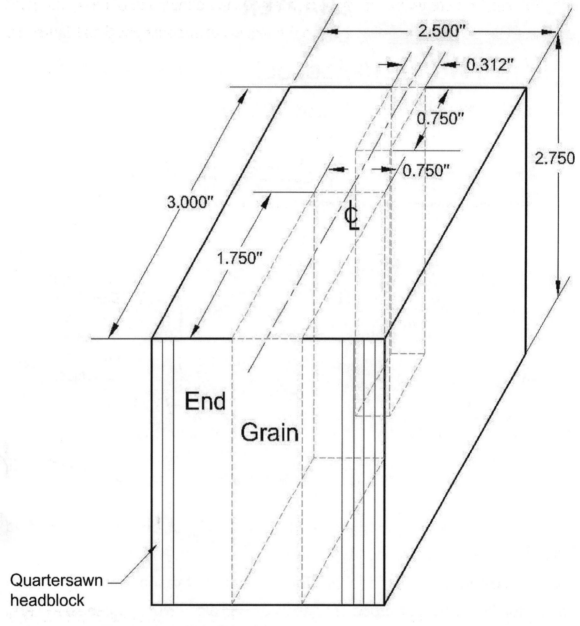

Figure 17 – Headblock

This way, the cut-out side and top and back will not be glued to the end grain of the headblock. It does not make a very strong joint. The top of the body <u>will</u> be, but the neck is installed over it, so it will strengthen this area.

Be sure the sides of the headblock are exactly square to each other. Now, referring to Figure 17 and Figure 19, cut a slot 3/4" wide x 1 3/4" deep in the A end. This is called a mortise and the tenon on the end of the neck will fit here. Figure out what width the neck is going to be at the 16th fret. My guitars are 2.130" wide at the 16th fret. The centerline of my neck matches the center line of the guitar itself so that everything is straight in line, so the slot is cut accordingly. See Figure 19.

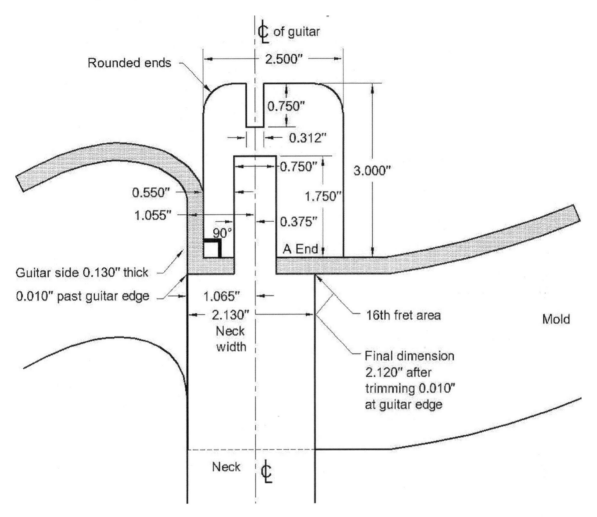

Figure 19 – Headblock Dimensions

The dimension from the mortise edge to the guitar edge is .550". This leaves .010" overhang in the cutout area to be trimmed after attaching the neck to the guitar. You can use a dado blade in your table saw or make multiple passes until your slot is .750". Or you can cut with a handsaw and chisel out the rest. Also, you can make a jig to clamp the headblock to while cutting. Be extremely careful when cutting the mortises in the head and tailblock. Tablesaws are famous for cutting off fingers! Once you cut the 3/4" mortise, cut a 5/16" slot in the other end on the centerline. Again, refer to Figure 19. Now round the front corners of the block and set it aside.

Now you are ready to make the tailblock. Cut your block 2.750" high x 2.500" wide x 1.500" long as per Figure 18.

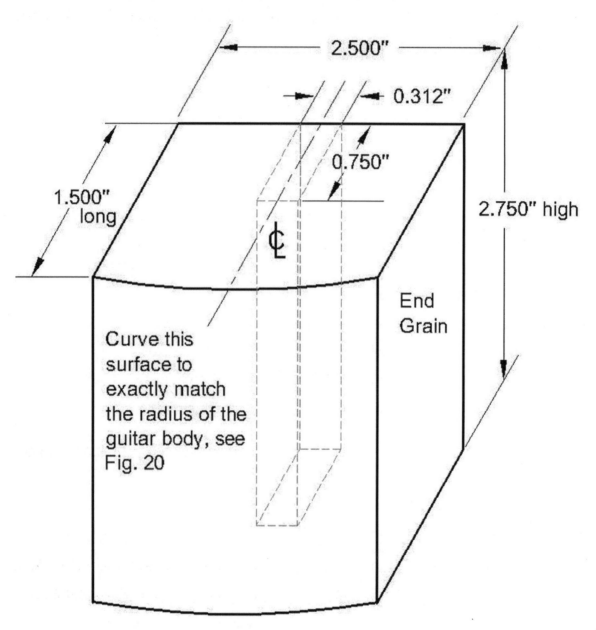

Figure 18 – Tailblock

Notice the orientation of the end grain again. The top, back and body will not be glued to the end grain. Arch the surface that the body will be glued to so that the surfaces match perfectly. Now cut a 5/16" wide slot by 3/4" deep exactly on centerline as in Figure 20.

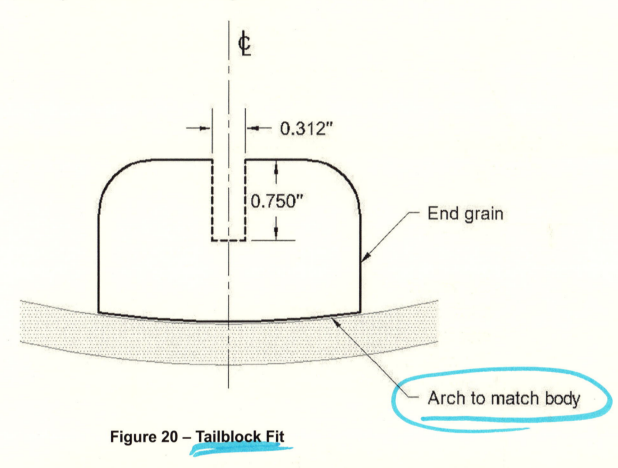

Figure 20 – Tailblock Fit

Again, round the front corners as you did to the headblock.

Now, with the body in the mold, place your headblock and tailblock in position on centerline and measure the length of the tone bar. See Figure 21.

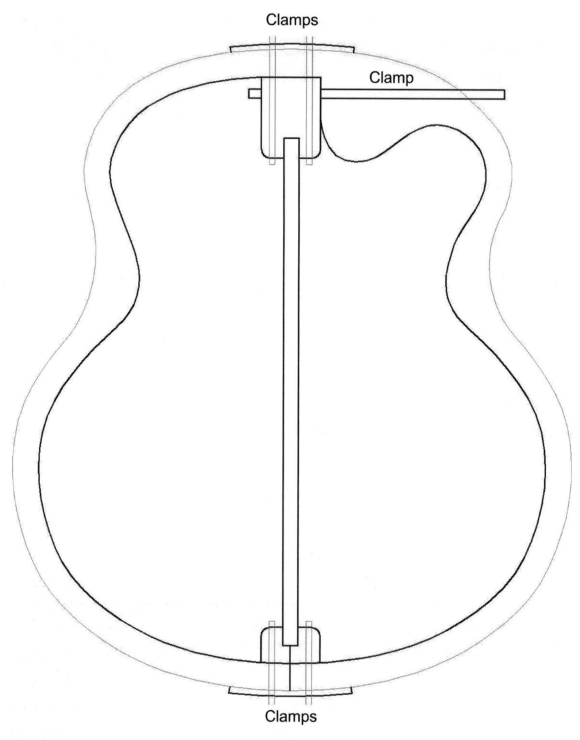

Figure 21 – Everything in Position

The tone bar should be made of maple, flatsawn so that when it is turned on edge, it becomes quartersawn. See Figure 22.

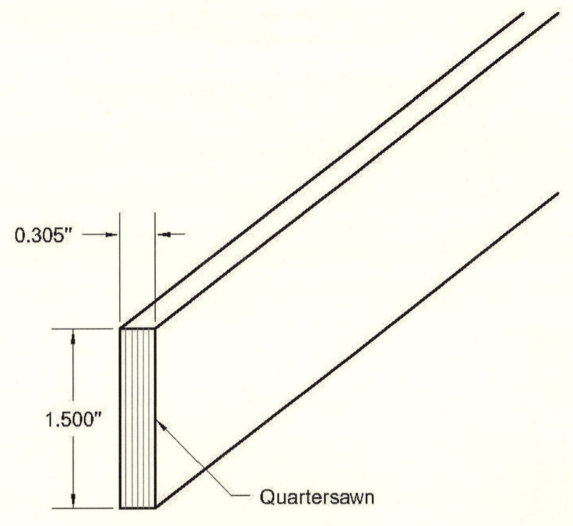

Figure 22 – Tone Bar

Cut the tone bar so that it is a snug fit end to end. Also, cut it .005" thinner than your slot to allow room for the glue. It should be .312" or so thick, 1 1/4" – 1 1/2" wide by however long to make a snug fit for length. The tone bar serves three purposes. First, it adds rigidity and stability to the guitar body. Second, it prevents the top of the guitar just in front of the neck in the area of the front pick-up and the top in the front of the bridge from sinking in, caused by the pull of the strings. Third, it cuts down on feedback just enough to give only a slight overtone warmth to the overall sound of the guitar. It does not touch the back or top of the guitar and effectively makes the neck one piece from the headstock to the butt of the guitar.

Before assembly, drill a (#12 drill) hole in the headblock 1/2" in from the end and 1/2" up from the bottom, per Figure 23.

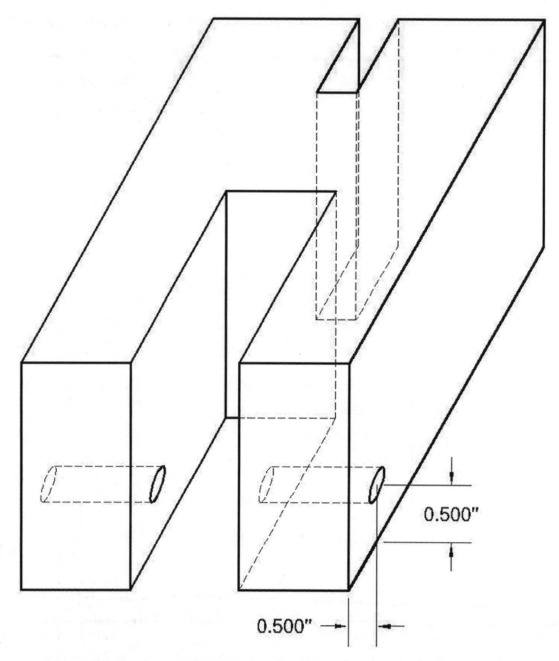

Figure 23 – Drill Nec-Loc Pin Hole

This is for a piece of 3/16" truss rod material, usually stainless that is installed later and forms part of the English Nec-Loc System. <u>You must drill this hole now before gluing the headblock in place</u>.

Now dry clamp everything in your mold to be sure of a good tight fit. When everything fits good, apply glue, clamp up and leave for one hour. Be sure the tone bar clears the back of the guitar by about 1/8". Wipe away any glue while wet with a damp rag. Install a 3/4" piece of plywood in the headblock mortise so that the clamps won't collapse the slot. See Figure 21, Photo 14B and 13.

Photo 13 – Glueing Up In Press

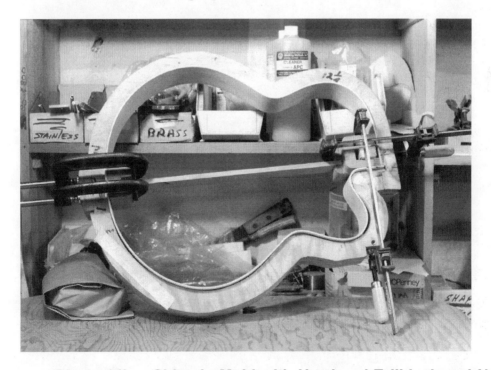

Photo 14b – Sides In Mold with Head and Tailblock and Nelson Tone Bar

Now you are ready to install the kerfing. I use mahogany kerfing and I buy it ready made in 30" strips. It is much easier and quicker than making my own.

We won't need to install any braces to the sides for strength as our sides are approximately 1/8" thick and laminated, making them very strong.

Remove the guitar body from the mold and make sure the glueing surfaces are cleaned of any contamination. For clamping the kerfing in place, I use clothespins with rubber bands wrapped around the lower part to make them stronger. It takes 80 - 100 per side. Slotted kerfing has a lot of give for installing in radiused areas.

The kerfing is the surface where the top and back of the guitar will be glued to. When you cut grooves later to install binding, you will be cutting a large portion of the top, back and side away, so the kerfing surface will hold everything together. Kerfing will break easily, so be careful. Apply a small bead of glue to the back flat area of the kerfing strip, spread evenly and press and clamp into place. Be careful to leave .010" or so sticking above the body surface to later be sanded down even. See Photo 14 & 14A.

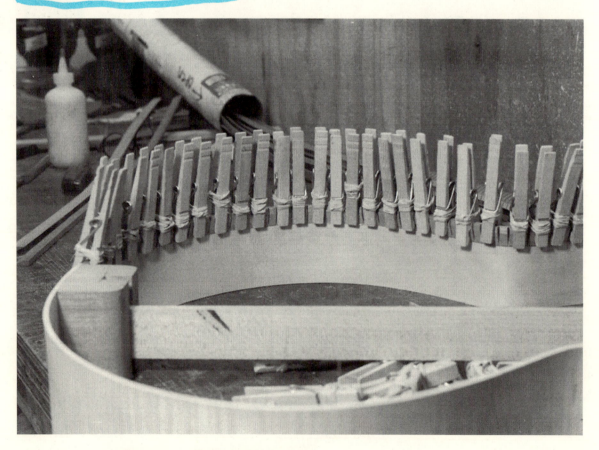

Photo 14 – Kerfing Glued In

Photo 14a – Kerfing Glued In

Wipe the excess glue away. If any of the surfaces fall below the level of the side, then the top or back won't glue up well enough, causing problems later. Clamp for one hour. When both sides are done and set for eight hours, sand them down even with the sides using your flat sanding surface.

Now that the rim assembly is finished, you are ready to install the back.

CHAPTER 6

INSTALLING THE BACK, STRAPBLOCK, PICKGUARD BRACKET BLOCK, JACK HOLE, NEC - LOC PIN, SPRAY LACQUER, LABEL

Check your back for being flat at the edges and mark the centerline on both sides. Also mark the centerline on the butt and top of the guitar body. Line up the back with the centerlines, and using the body as a template, trace the outline on the inside face of the back. Trim to this line and remove burrs with sandpaper or a file.

I use spool clamps for assembly. You can purchase these from Stewart McDonald. Pre-clamp to be sure of a good fit. Put a small bead of glue on the body back - side kerfing, spread evenly and install the back. See Photo 15.

Photo 15 - Back Clamped

Leave the clamps on for one hour. Remove any glue on the inside and leave set for 8 hours. Trim the back even with the sides using a file and sandpaper.

I make the strapblock and pickguard bracket block out of maple. Screws into maple won't work loose or be a source of weakness. The strapblock is 1" square by 3/8" thick, contoured to fit the inside curve at the upper bout by the neck. It is installed in the center, 2½" from the centerline of the guitar. Glue up and clamp for 1 hour. Be sure to use a rubber or wooden caul on the outside to prevent marking the body. See Photo 16 and Figure 24.

Photo 16 - Strap Block Installed

44

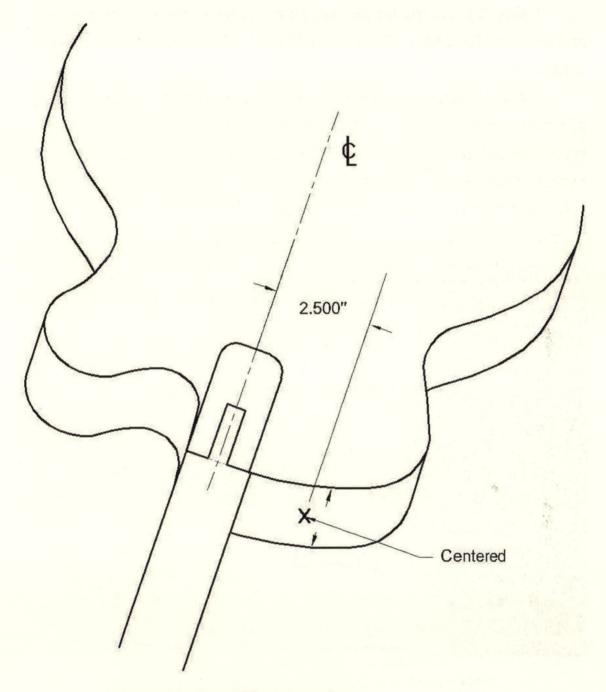

Figure 24 - Strap Block Location

The pickguard bracket block is also 1" square by 3/8" thick and is contoured to fit. It is installed 6" from the top of the cut away. See Figure 25.

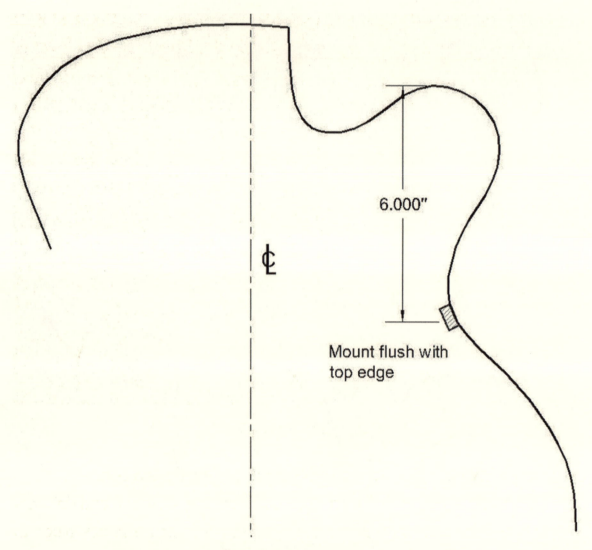

Figure 25 - Pickguard Block Location

It is installed even with the top. You have to remove a few pieces of kerfing to do this, or you may install this block when you install the kerfing. See Photo 17.

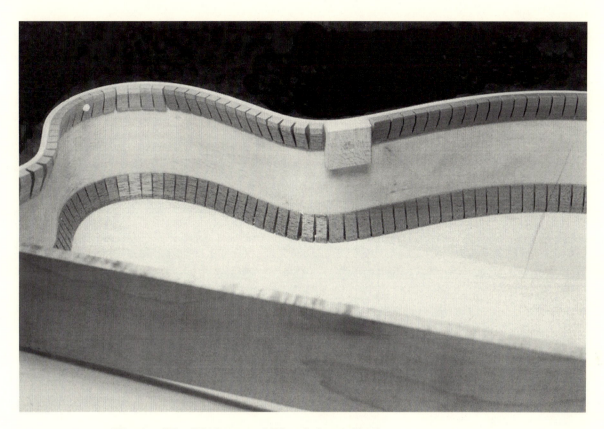

Photo 17 - Pickguard Block Installed

Glue up and clamp for 1 hour. Sand even with the top edge.

Locate the jack hole 6" from the butt centerline. Center it and drill with a 3/8" bradpoint drill bit. Drill carefully and use a contoured back block to prevent chipping. See Figure 26.

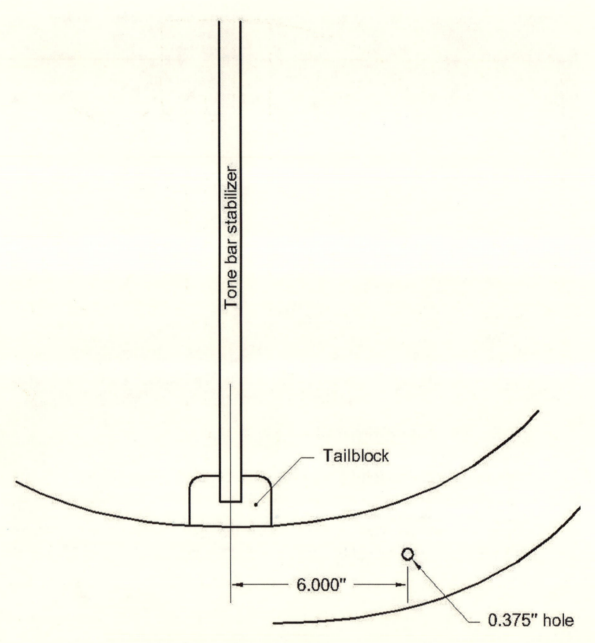

Figure 26 - Jack Hole Location

Install the nec-loc pin. Use a piece of 3/16" stainless truss rod material. I put a drop or two of glue on it before I push it in, but this is not necessary. It isn't going anywhere.

Locate your label at this point if you have one, or some means of identification and install it so it can be seen through the base side F-hole. See Figure 27.

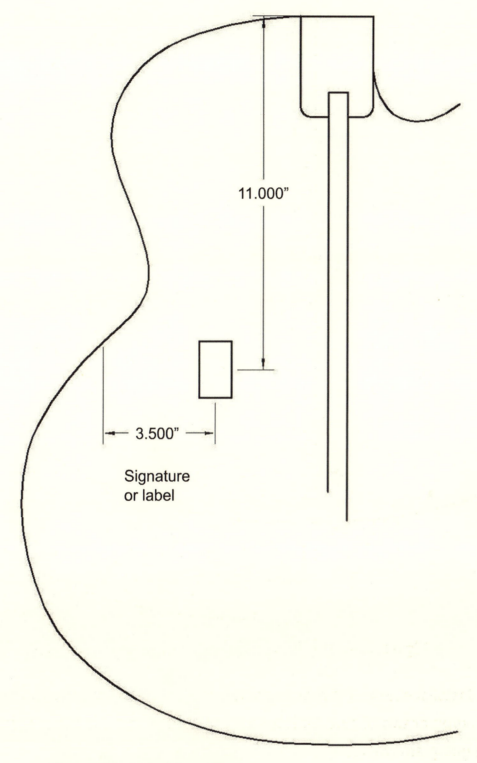

Figure 27 - Label Location

Now tape off the top of the kerfing in preparation for spraying the inside of the guitar body. This will be the glueing surface when you install the top and you don't want any finish on it to interfere with the glue. I spray two dry coats of clear lacquer. This does not completely prevent the absorption of moisture, but it will slow it down. It will also add to the overall tonal quality of the guitar.

You are now ready to make the neck. Lay the body aside in a safe place and cover it to keep it clean and dust free.

CHAPTER 7

MAKING THE NECK

I gave the neck of the guitar a great deal of thought and research as to the method of joining it to the body. I have an older guitar that the neck joint has loosened up on and I was determined to not have that happen to the guitars that I make. It is a very common problem and I have come up with a method that prevents it. It had to be a strong joint with a good amount of glueing surface, immovable but with the ability to disassemble in the case of future repairs. I call it the English Nec-Loc System. It works very well. I am currently working on a patent for the idea.

Necks can be made out of several different kinds of material and in several different ways. They can be one piece or laminated of several pieces. Acoustic guitars usually have mahogany necks, whether steel or nylon stringed. Steel stringed guitars usually have maple necks. As of late, there are also composite necks being made of carbon laminated with wood or even aluminum.

Using the right wood and correct construction techniques is very important. Try to obtain the very best wood available. You can sometimes find great wood at your local lumber yard but you are better off buying properly dried wood from suppliers who specialize in just that. See the suppliers list in the Appendix.

A beautiful looking guitar adds up to a big fat zero if the neck is not good. Bad necks have ruined and discouraged more guitar players than you can count. What I am trying to say here is that the neck needs all of your skill and attention possible. The neck needs to be right.

The neck that I make is the laminated type. Starting with flatsawn stock is alright because when it is turned on edge, it becomes quartersawn in the correct orientation. See Figure 28 also Figure 1 & 2.

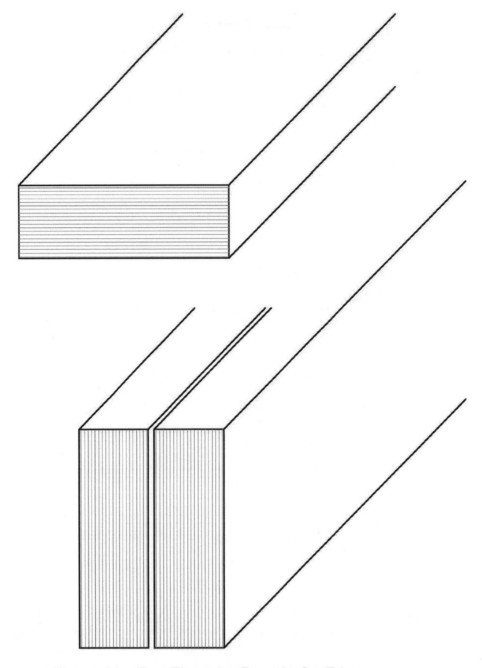

Figure 28 – Two Flatsawn Boards On Edge

If you are going to make more than one guitar, it would be better to make a pattern. See Figure 29 for dimensions.

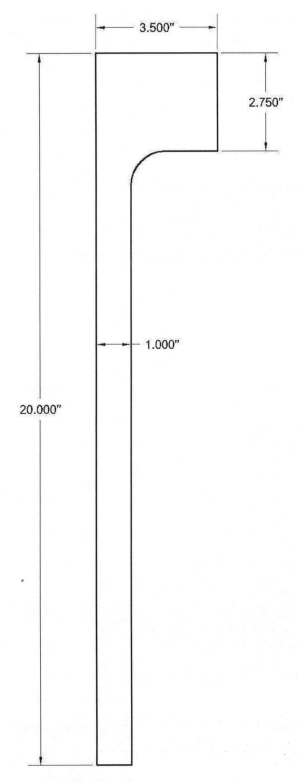

Figure 29 – Neck Pattern

These may vary depending on what you decide to make. Start with a board that is planed or sanded to the final dimension of 1 1/4" thick by 4" or 5" wide and however long it needs to be for your neck. Mark the pattern twice on the board and cut on a bandsaw. See Figure 30.

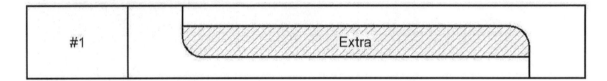

Figure 30 – Marking Neck Pattern on Board

A wide enough board allows the pieces to match for pattern and color. Now cut a piece of .080" black (gaboon) ebony to the same pattern. Glue the three pieces together with the ebony in the center. Be sure that the glued surfaces are perfectly flat before glueing so as not to build in any stress. Remove the clamps in a hour or so and let dry for 24 hours. Using your flat sanding surface or a jointer, flatten the top surface of the neck. You might find a cabinet shop in your area who can do this for a small cost. Also, you don't have to put the ebony piece in the neck. This is the way I make mine, your ideas may be different.

My neck joint consists of a mortise and tenon with a lock system. Using your combination square, set your table saw mitre at 4° and cut the heel end of the neck at a 4° angle. See Figure 31.

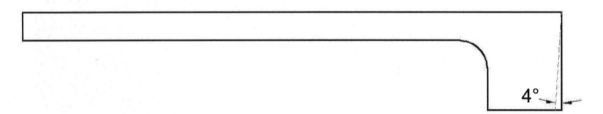

Figure 31 – Cut End At 4° Angle

The tenon could be cut with a good dovetail saw but it is cleaner and more accurate when done on a table saw. The tenon is 1 3/4" long and 3/4" wide. The side cuts are done first at a 4° angle matching the heel cut you already made. Set the table saw blade at a 3° angle and using the mitre fence set at 4° make the two cuts as in Photo 18 & 18A.

Photo 18 – Making Side Cuts On Table Saw

Photo 18a – Finished Cuts

The vertical stop in the picture assures the same distance from the end on both sides. Now, standing the neck on end, cut the width to 3/4" and the depth to meet your side cuts. See Figure 32 and Photo 19 & 19A.

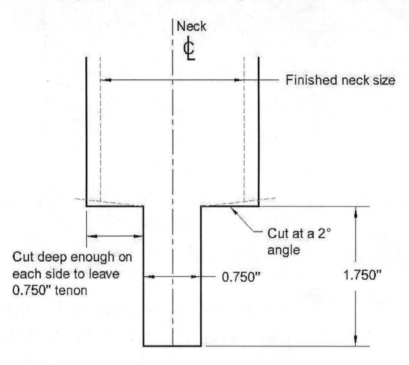

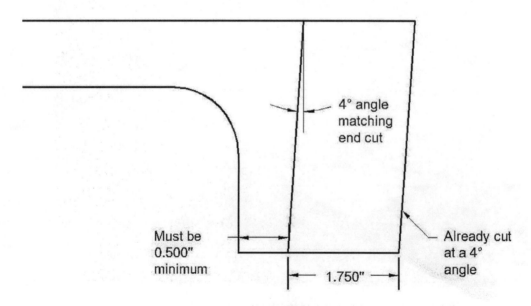

Figure 32 – Cutting Tenon On Neck

Photo 19 – Making Vertical Cuts

Again, this can be done by hand. Now measure back 13 5/8" from the body contact point at the heel. At this line, draw a 15° angle line along the side. This is where the head will be glued, allowing the neck to join the body at the 16th fret. You can make these cuts on the table saw using a jig for this purpose. See Figure 33.

Photo 19a – Finished Tenon

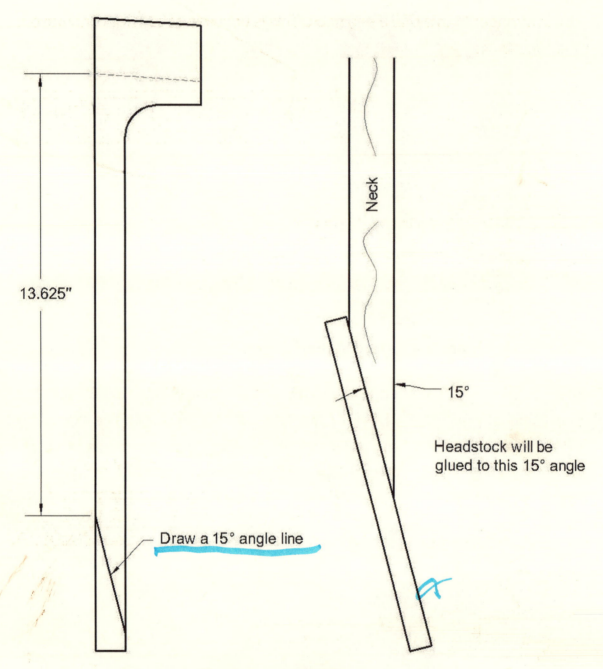

Figure 33 – Cutting 15° Angle On Neck

Make sure your cut is square across the top of the neck. Now we make the headstock.

Decide on the headstock shape that you want. There are many different ones and sometimes you can tell who made the guitar by the shape of the headstock. I glue my headstock onto the neck as in Figure 33 because this joint is stronger than a one piece neck. This is because of the grain orientation. See Figure 34.

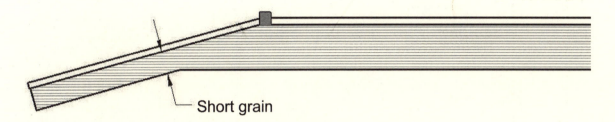

One piece neck and headstock
Notice the short grain in the headstock
The short grain area is a weak spot

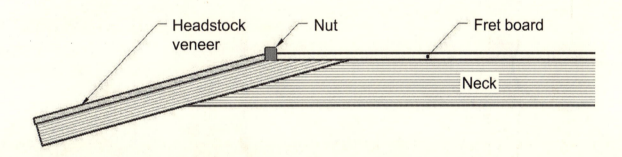

This is a much stronger type of construction than the above

Figure 34 – Headstock Joint Orientation

Be sure to start with quartersawn stock if possible. Curly maple is very hard to find in quartersawn stock. It should be 4 1/2" x 10 1/2". Thin it to .475. Adding a .150 veneer to the top of the headstock gives a final thickness of .625 which is perfect for the tuners I use. Be sure of the thickness requirements of the tuners you will use before you thin the headstock. Now cut it in half lengthwise and add a .080 thick piece of ebony between to match the neck.

Be sure to hold it flat while glueing. Remove clamps in 1 hour and let set for 24 hours. Sand flat on both sides. Lay it on the neck as in Photo 20 and Figure 35.

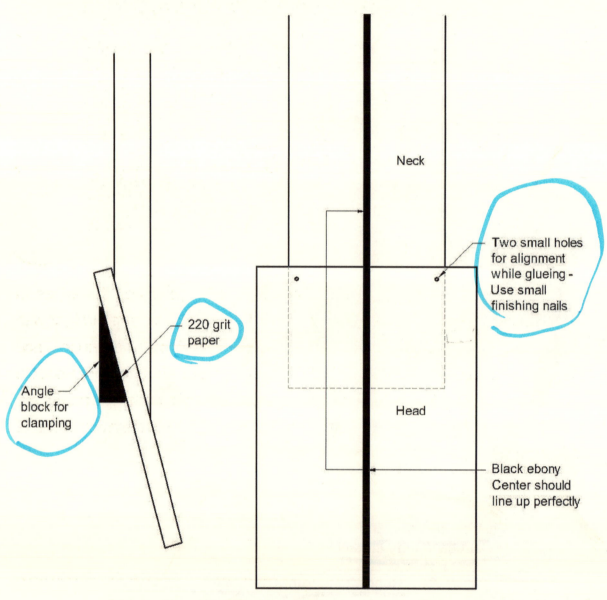

Figure 35 – Aligning Headstock

Photo 20 Glueing Headstock to Neck

Drill two small locating holes for 1 1/4" finishing nails on the edges to hold it in alignment for glueing. Be sure that the ebony lines are straight with each other. Apply glue in both surfaces, use nails to align and clamp in place for 1 hour. One angle block with 220 grit paper on one side held with double stick tape allows good clamping. See Figure 35. Remove clamps and leave for 24 hours. File or sand the headstock excess to match the neck surface. See Figure 36.

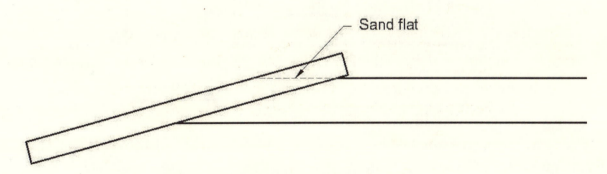

Figure 36 – Cut and Sand Headstock

Now cut the rabbit on the heel end of the neck for the finger board extension piece as in Figure 37.

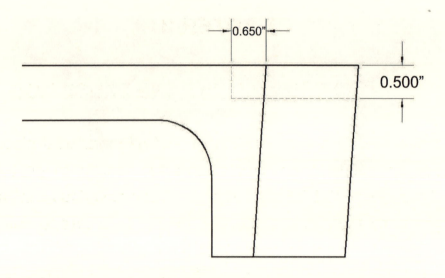

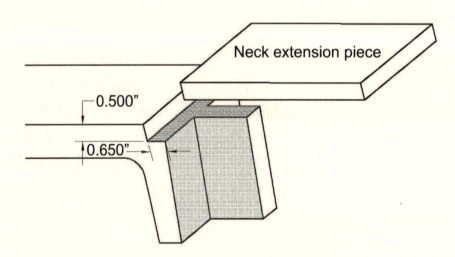

Figure 37 – Cutting Rabbit On Neck End

Use a piece of maple from the same board that you cut your neck pieces from so that they match. Cut it 2 1/2" wide x 1/2" thick x 5" long. This can be done by router, by hand or using your table saw. Again the fit must be perfect as the joint will show on the sides of the neck.

When it fits exactly, glue up and clamp for 1 hour. Let set 24 hours. Now sketch on your head shape and rough trim. Leave excess, especially in the nut and first fret area for final sizing later. Now flatten the top of the neck for its entire length, using your flat sanding table. At this point, we are ready to install the truss rod, covered in Chapter 8.

CHAPTER 8

MAKING AND INSTALLING THE TRUSS ROD

Because necks have gotten thinner and narrower, and steel strings exert a lot of force, causing the neck to bow away from the stings, the use of a truss rod has become standard. They have been of various configurations over the years, mostly non-adjustable, from oval to square to double, etc. Most modern guitars contain an adjustable type.

Inserted into a groove in the top of the neck, they add stiffness and the ability to adjust some of the bow out of the neck. Not all however, because some bow is necessary to allow for the vibration of the strings. But never use the truss rod for string height adjustment.

My truss rod is anchored at both ends. It has a slight bow in it. One end has a nut which can be tightened or loosened. Tightening puts the neck under compression. The rod is installed as deeply as possible within the neck so that there is more wood above the rod than below. When the nut is tightened, more compression is taking place below the truss rod than above causing the neck to bow toward the stings, counteracting their pull. Bear this in mind later when we get to the fretboard. The fretboard adds considerable strength and mass above the truss rod. See Figure 38A for the configuration of my truss rod.

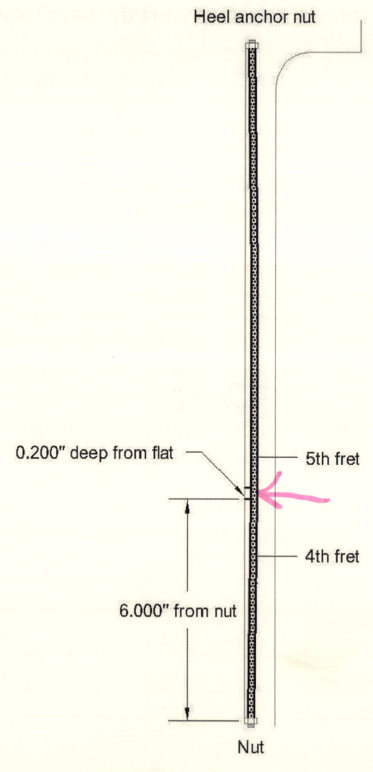

Figure 38a – Bending Truss Rod

My truss rod is designed with the anchor at the heel and the adjustable nut in the headstock. The slot has its deepest point between the 4th and 5th fret. This can be done with a special tool and a jig as in Bob Benedetto's book on page 84. See Figure 38.

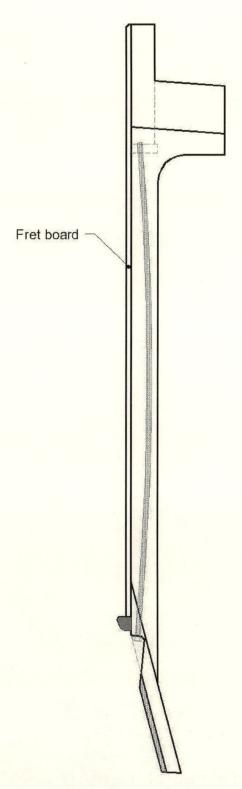

Figure 38 – Truss Rod Slot

KEEP NECK STRAIGHT & SQUARE UNTIL MUCH LATER.

It can also be done on a table saw which results in a straight slot. It can be done with a router and a special jig clamped in a vise. See Photo 21 & 21A.

TAPERED STRIPS FOR CURVED TRUSS ROD

Photo 21 – Truss Rod Slot Cutting Jig

Photo 21a – Truss Rod Slot Cutting Jig

I use a 3/16 carbide router bit rounded at the end. I made a small jig which clamps onto the router base. It is simple and works very well. See Photo 22 & 22a & 22b.

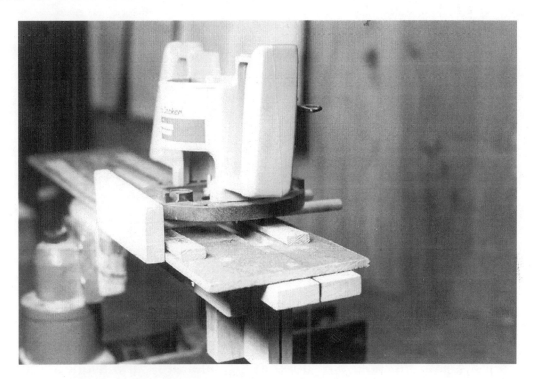

Photo 22 – Router Set-Up

Photo 22a – Router Set-Up

Photo 22b – Router Set-Up

First drill a 3/8" hole 5/8" deep in the heel area at a slight angle. The front of the 3/8" hole should just touch the line where the neck extension piece is glued in. See Figure 39.

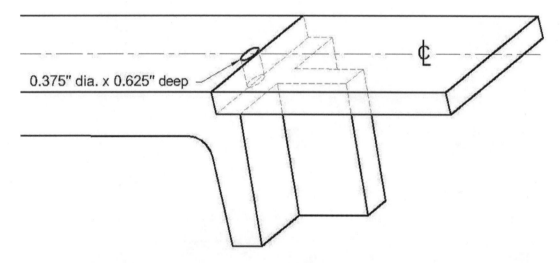

Figure 39 – Anchor Hole for Truss Rod

Measure 6" from the front of the nut and mark the top of the neck. This is the point between the 4th and 5th fret. See Figure 40.

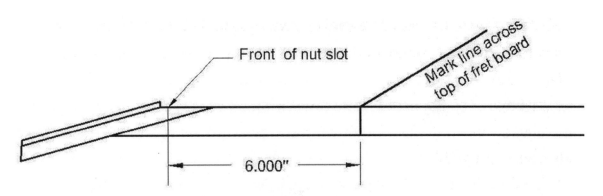

Figure 40 – Marking Between 4th and 5th Fret

Set your jig on top, locating the deepest cut at that mark. Starting at the 3/8" hole, rout out past the nut area and .300 deep at the back of the nut. See Figure 41.

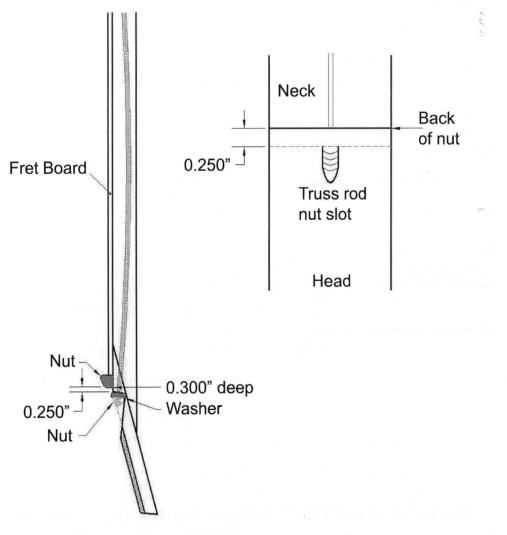

Figure 41 – Truss Rod Specs

Make sure the slot is exactly centered on the neck by adjusting the router jig accordingly. Remember, this slot can be cut on a table saw. You can't maintain the .400 depth however because that will be too deep at the nut, so you will have to compensate. Slots are still done this way and they will work just fine. Just be very careful around the table saw. It doesn't know the difference between wood and fingers!

I use a 3/16" stainless rod that I purchase at a hardware store and bend it to match my curved slot. See Figure 38A. Cut a piece of 3/8" stainless rod 5/8" long and file a flat area on it. Drill a #19 hole from the flat area through the rod and tap the hole with a 10-32 tap. See Figure 42.

0.375" stock 0.625" long
File flat - Drill #19 hole
Tap with 10-32

Figure 42 – Drilling 0.375 Stock

Be sure to have enough threaded rod at the headstock end for the nut and a thick washer. See Figure 43.

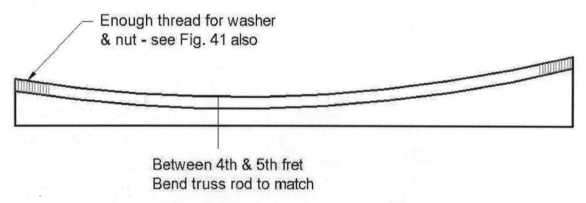

Figure 43 – Bend and Thread .188 Truss Rod

I use a standard 5/16" brass Gibson style nut. In the case of overtightening, the brass nut should strip before the rod breaks. This is not always true, however. Many people not understanding the use of the truss rod have broken them from overtightening, causing a very expensive repair!

Now clamp your neck in the vise and cut the adjusting nut slot with a 1/2" rotary file and drill 1/4" back from the back of the nut as in Photo 23 and Figure 41.

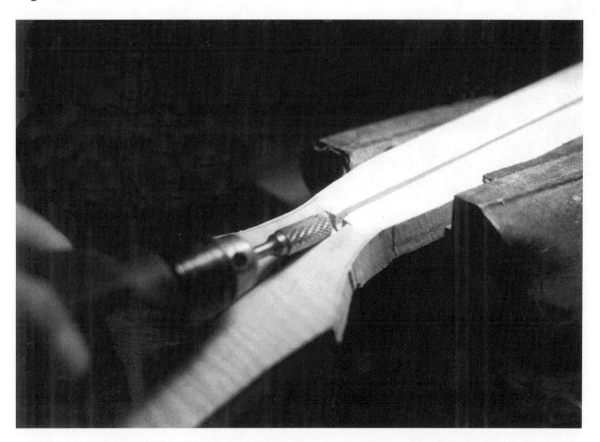

Photo 23 – Cutting Truss Rod Nut Slot in Headstock

Go just deep enough so that you can get the adjusting wrench on the nut. The wrench I use is from Stewart McDonald Supply. Remember when doing this that you are weakening the neck and headstock joint so be careful to go just deep enough so that when the head stock veneer is glued on, the nut will be just below the surface so that it won't touch the truss rod nut cover when it is installed.

Now make a filler from maple or ebony that will be installed above the truss rod. It should stick above the surface of the neck a little bit. It should be .005 - .008 thinner than the slot to allow for glue on the sides.

Now apply epoxy to the threads at the heal end of the truss rod and put a little epoxy in the 3/8" hole. Thread the 3/8" rod that you drilled and tapped onto the heel end and install the truss rod, pushing it down into the slot firmly. Put yellow glue on both sides of your filler piece, fit it into the slot and clamp firmly. See Photo 24.

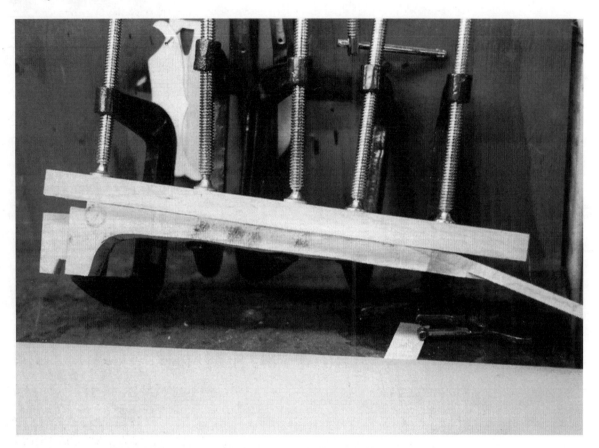

Photo 24 – Clamping Truss Rod Slot Filler

Do not put glue on the truss rod or in the slot itself and do not over clamp. The truss rod must be free to move with adjustment or it won't work. Also, it should fit snug enough in the slot so that it does not rattle and cause a buzz. If you want you can cut 1/4" truss rod slot and wrap the 3/16" truss rod with filament tape until the fit is snug, but I have not had any problems doing it the above described way. Remove the clamps in 1 hour and let set 24 hours. File or sand the filler piece flat with the neck surface. Now double check to make sure the neck is flat its full length.

CHAPTER 9

FRETBOARDS

Like the rest of the guitar, fretboards can be made of several different materials. Three most common are ebony, rosewood, and maple. I use ebony because it is a beautiful black color (gaboon), is very stable, dense, and makes a good background for mother of pearl inlays. It will wear better than a softer material and adds strength to the neck.

Ebony can be expensive and must be properly dried to be any good. Try to obtain quartersawn wood. Without a good background in this area, it is difficult to do this on your own. Your best bet starting out is to go to a reputable dealer who specializes in this area. Look in the Appendix for a list of suppliers.

Start with 1/4" thick ebony wood. You could at this point set up and cut your own fret slots, but take my advice. There are folks out there who will cut your fret slots by computer for just a few dollars. This is an area where precision is a must. Before you make the decision to do this yourself, I suggest that you read Mr. Hideo Kamimoto's book, Complete Guitar Repair on Equal Tempered Tuning, and Bob Benedetto's book, Making an Archtop Guitar, on making the finger board so you will understand the importance of accuracy. A mistake of just .010 of an inch can make a difference. I suggest that first timers have it done.

I decided on a 25" scale length for my guitars. It's in-between the short (24¾") and long (25½") scales. Long scales are better suited for players who use the upper registers of the neck, say from the 14th to the 20th fret. The distance between frets in this area is larger. However, the distance between frets 1 through 6 is also larger, making it difficult for the average player to make chords there. On shorter scales, it is difficult for players to use the upper register because of the closeness of the frets. So I find that the 25" scale is the best of both worlds, so to speak.

So begin with a new fretboard that has been slotted to a 25" scale with .022 slot width and 22 frets. Establish the center at each end and mark the center point with a sharp scribe. Put a .022 feeler gage into the first fret slot and scribe a line parallel to it and .200 from it. This is where the front of the nut will be. Do the same at the 22nd fret, only mark .300 from it. Trim both ends exactly to the marked lines. See Figure 44.

My neck is 1.735 wide at the nut and 2.150 at the 16th fret. Yours may vary from this according to your dimensions. Measure out from the centerline exactly 1/2 of 1.735 at the nut end and ½ of 2.150 at the 16th fret, minus .100 on each side. This allows for .100 thick binding on each side of the fretboard. Using a straight edge, scribe these lines and trim exactly to them. Be sure all sides are square with the bottom of the board. See Figure 45.

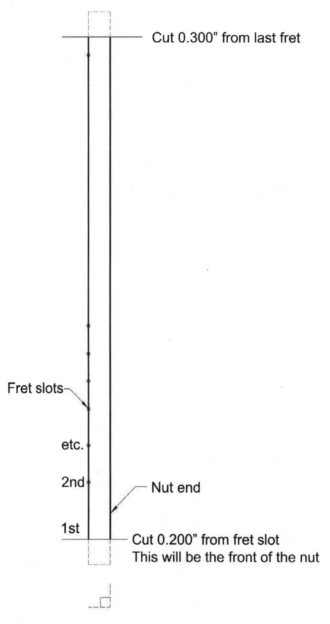

Figure 44 & 45 – Cutting Fretboard Ends

Now you are ready to put the radius on the fretboard. Mine are radiused to 14". You could have it done by the company that cuts the fret slots for you or you can buy a radius block and do it yourself. I use a 14" radius block that is 8" long. I spray it with a light coat if 3M Adhesive #77 Super, wait one minute and put on #50 or #80 grit paper. This assures an accurate radius. Lay the fretboard on a flat surface and secure it with a piece of double stick tape at each end. Also put a 3/4" – 1" thick straight edge next to it so that the edge is parallel with the centerline of the fretboard. The distance between the parallel lines should be 1/2 the width of your radius block. In my case, this is 11/2". Your radius block will locate and slide along the side of the straight edge to ensure an accurate radius. Make a chalk line down the centerline of the fretboard and as you are sanding, when you start to remove the chalkline, change to #120 grit, then to #220 grit, then to #400 grit. Be sure to sand with even pressure the full length of the fretboard so that the edge thickness is the same on each side. Also try not to thin the center less than .240. This helps add maximum strength to the neck. See Figure 46.

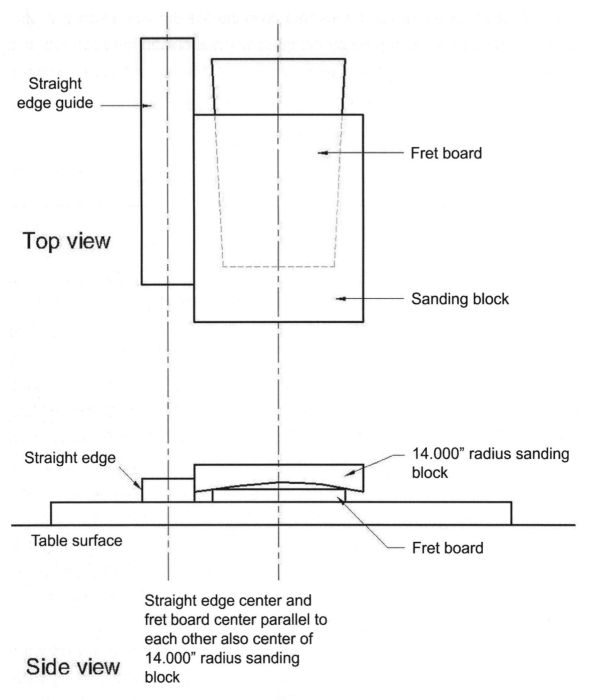

Figure 46 – Shaping Fretboard

Now you must resaw the fret slots to ensure adequate depth so the fretwire will seat properly. For this you can buy a fret saw the same width as your fret slot. Be sure to use the saw in a pulling motion instead of pushing or you could chip the edge of the fretboard. Before you do this, chamfer the fretslot edges with a small triangular file. You do this for several reasons. It helps start the frets easier; it prevents chipping the top when you use your fretting saw and it helps prevent chipping when it comes time for you or a repairman to refret the guitar. Chips can be glued back in place by using a drop of super glue and re-sand. See Figure 47.

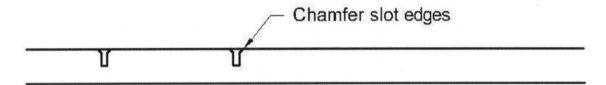

Figure 47 – Fret Slots To Correct Depth

At this point, you can install your inlays or you can do it after you glue the fretboard onto the neck. There are several good books on how to do inlay work. It would be a good idea to study these and practice on scrap before you attempt to do your fretboard. You can also install round dots after drilling the holes with an appropriate size drill. Inlays are usually done in the space between the 2nd and 3rd fret, the 4th and 5th fret, 6th and 7th fret, 8th and 9th fret, 11th and 12th fret (usually two here), 14th and 15th fret and the 16th and 17th fret. The inlays can be almost anything. Mine match my 'F' hole shape and so they are part of my signature. I suggest on your first guitar, try round dots. You can buy these already made in several sizes. Set two, evenly spaced between the 11th and 12th fret. Drill your holes .050 deep and use .060 thick mother of pearl, abalone, or the material of your choice. Use black epoxy to install and when dry, file or sand even with the fretboard surface, maintaining the 14th radius. Smooth to #600 grit and smooth the inlays to #1000 grit.

Now you are ready to install the initial binding before glueing the fretboard to the neck. I use .020 ivoroid / .020 black / .060 ivoroid theme on my neck binding. The total thickness is .100. I install the ivoroid / black .020 / .020 first. Then after glueing the fretboard to the neck, I install the .060 invoroid. Use Weld-on #1802 for the cement. In my opinion, it is the best.

The end piece is installed first with the ends mitred. Then, mitre the ends of the side pieces. Lay a small bead of cement on the binding and hold in place for a minute or so until it sets and leave to dry for 24 hours. Sand or file the binding flush with the bottom of the fret board. Do the same with the top, maintaining the 14" radius. See Figure 48.

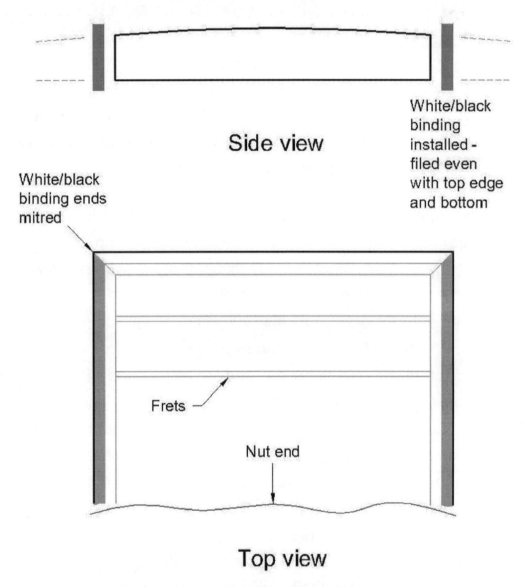

Figure 48 – Installing Black/White Binding

Now saw through the binding with your fret saw at each fret slot. Again, be sure to saw on the pull instead of the push in order to prevent breaking the binding loose.

CHAPTER 10

INSTALLING THE HEADSTOCK VENEER, FRETBOARD AND FRETS

Lay a straight edge down the center of the ebony line on the surface of the neck and draw a line from where the ebony ends to the end of the neck extension. This is for locating the fretboard. See Figure 49

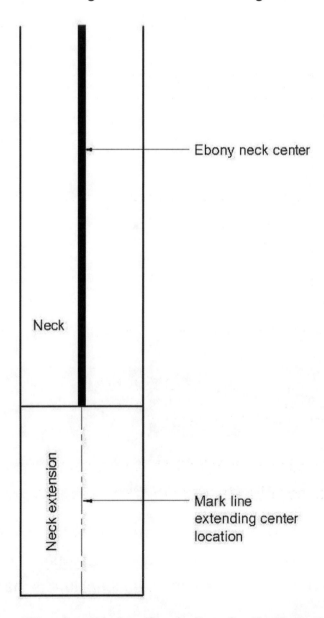

Figure 49 – Continuing Centerline On Fretboard Extension Piece

An alternative way is to cut the neck extension piece in half (before glueing it in place) and add an .080 thick piece of ebony in the center like you did with the headstock. This also adds a touch of class to your guitar.

The next step is to glue on the headstock veneer. I use the same material as the outer veneer of the guitar body so that it is more consistent for looks. Other material can be used such as black ebony, all colors of plastic, etc. Some of these make installing a logo much easier. Since I use wood, trying to do a good inlay is next to impossible so I inlay a black ebony oval shaped piece first. Then I inlay my mother of pearl into the ebony. See Photo 25.

Photo 25 – Headstock Logo Inlay

Whichever veneer you decide on, remember that it has to be .150 thick if you thinned the headstock to .475. This gives you a finished thickness of .625. This works very well for the Grover Imperial tuners that I use.

First, trim the headstock to your lines, keeping in mind the nut area width of 1.735. File the nut end of the veneer at 15° angle as in Figure 50.

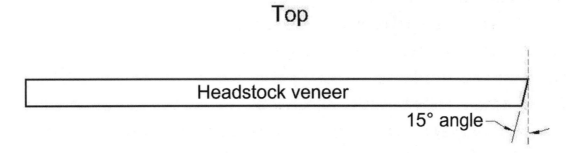

Figure 50 – Cutting Headstock Veneer

Also locate and cut your truss rod hole in the veneer to match the headstock truss rod slot. Finish form it with files so that the truss rod wrench fits easily.

Make sure the veneer and headstock are flat. Glue on the veneer, centering it exactly. Be sure to use wooden cauls on both sides for clamping to prevent damage to both surfaces. Be sure that the 15° angle edge is located exactly where the flat portion of the neck and the 15° angle of the headstock intersect. This will be the back locating surface of the nut. See Figure 51.

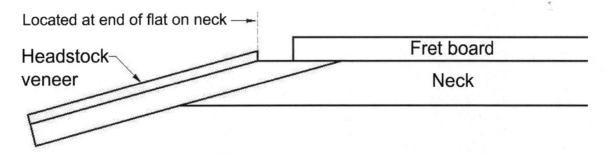

Figure 51 – Veneer Location

Clamp for 1 hour, then let set for 24 hours. Now trim exactly even with the headstock. See Photo 26.

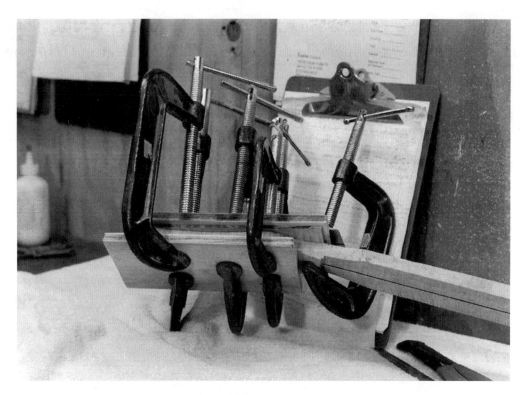

Photo 26 – Glueing Headstock Veneer

At this point, you are ready to cut the headstock binding grooves. These must be cut before installing the fretboard so that the router will clear. Use the same router set-up that you used for body binding. I do the same binding on the headstock that I do on the body for consistency and aesthetics. This time, the purfling cut can be the same depth that the outer .060 binding grove is. I cut to a depth that allows a small portion of binding under the nut as in Figure 52.

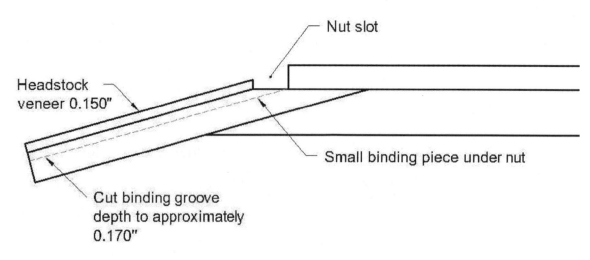

Figure 52 – Cutting Headstock Binding Grooves

I go .170 down and the same thickness as the binding (.100). Clean the grooves and file any fuzziness smooth. Be sure to maintain the outer edges square. Don't round them off as you clean the grooves. See Figure 53.

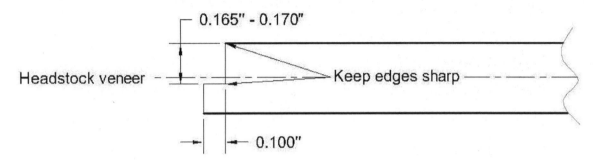

Figure 53 – Binding Grooves Dimensions

Now drill a small hole in the 3rd fret inlay cavity and also in the 17th cavity of the fretboard the same size as a small finishing nail. I use a 3/16" nut that I buy from Stew Mac. I thin them to .170 – .175. Set the nut in place and locate the fretboard exactly centered and up tight against the nut. Clamp it down and install two small nails in the inlay holes you drilled, tapping them in lightly.

Apply glue to the fretboard bottom and install, tapping the nails slightly. Clip these nails off, leaving enough to grip with pliers later to remove after the glue is dry. Clamp using 14" R sanding blocks. Drill small holes to fit over the nails ends, remove clamps in 1 – 1 1/2 hours. Clean the glue out of what will become the binding grooves with a sharp chisel being careful not to damage the wood or the binding on the fretboard. Figure 54.

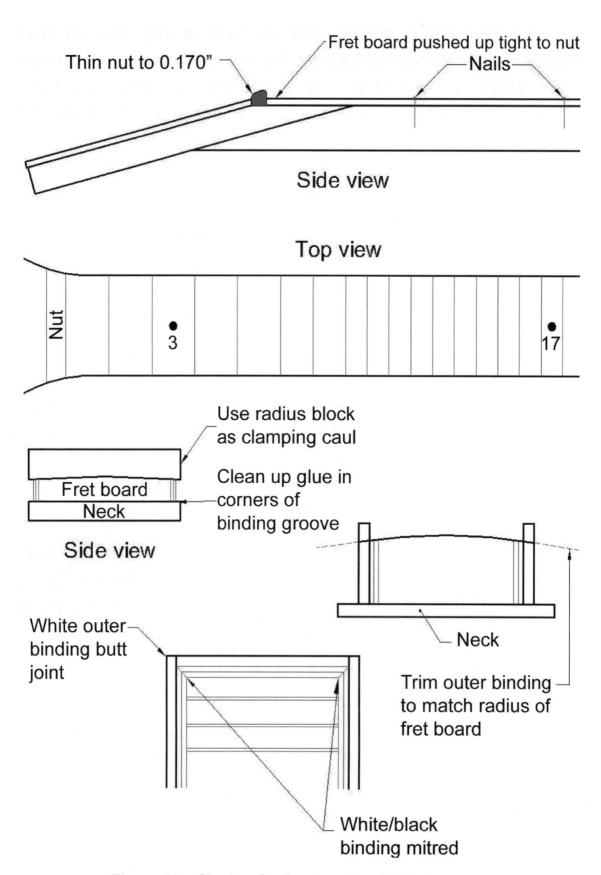

Figure 54 – Glueing On Fretboard and Binding

The next step is to install the headstock binding. Use the same combination as the body and the neck. The trick here is to mitre the corners. Make sure the binding groove is cleaned and the outer edges are square. I dip my binding in boiling water, wipe it dry and quickly fit it to the groove and hold it until it cools. Cut the pieces long so you will be able to file the ends of the top to fit as in Figure 57 and 58.

Figure 57 & 58 – Installing Headblock Binding

Tape this piece in place while you fit the side pieces to match, leaving them long enough to go to the front of the nut slot. When they fit perfectly, glue in place and tape. I use masking tape. Remove the tape in one hour and let the glue cure for 24 – 36 hours before sanding and scraping. See Photo 27.

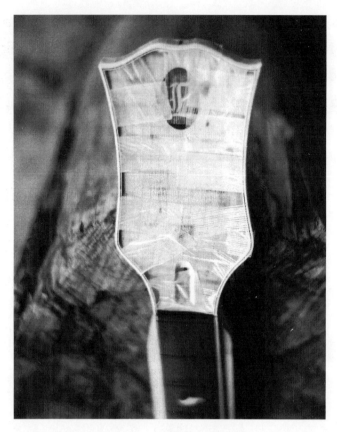

Photo 27 – Glueing Headstock Binding

Now scrape or sand flat with the edges and the top of the headstock. Be sure not to thin out the outer binding. File the binding even with the bottom of the nut slot, leaving a slight triangular shape as in Figure 59 and 52.

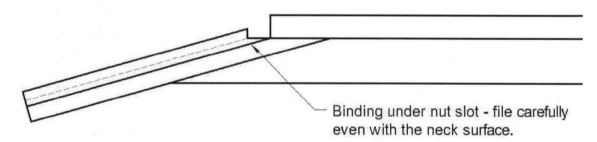

Figure 59 – Binding Location

If you have not installed your fretboard inlays, do so now.

Install the .060 outer white binding on the fretboard using the same glue as before. This time, the joint at the end of the fretboard will be a lap, not a mitre. Apply a small bead of glue and hold the binding in place until set. Let set 24 hours. Then scrape and sand to the 14" fretboard. See Figure 55 & 56.

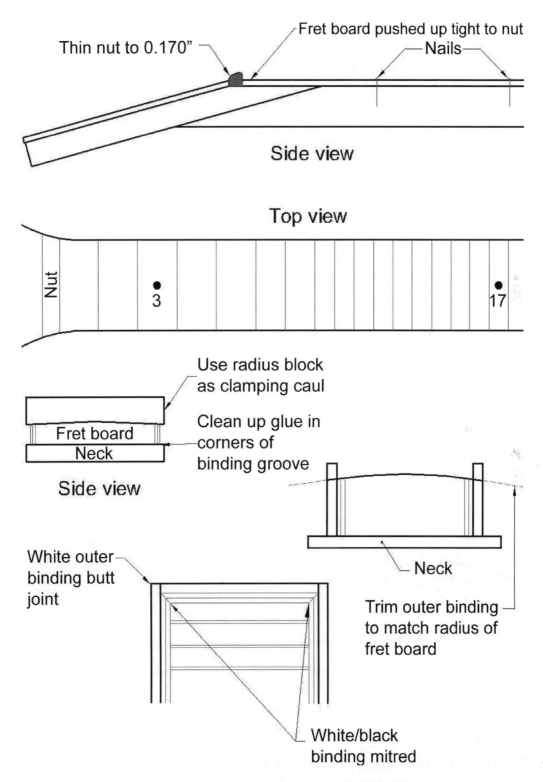

Figure 55 – Glueing On Fretboard and Binding

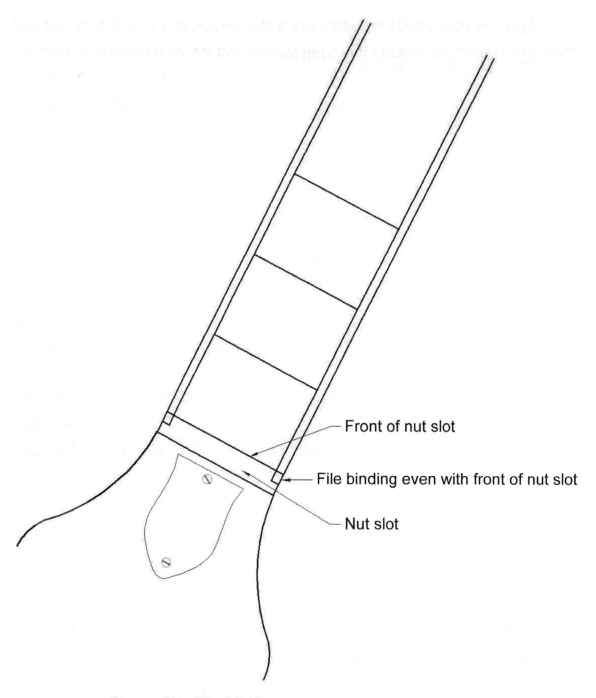

Figure 56 – File Binding

Also file or sand your fret board inlays even with the fretboard top and to 1000 grit if you have not already done so.

Now, rebevel the tops of the fret slots using a small triangular file as before. Clean out the fret slots carefully, right up to but not including the white binding.

You are now ready to install the frets. Check that your inlays are still good. Do any further work at this point like checking for pin holes in the epoxy, beveling of the slots, etc. Be sure not to round over the edges of the fretboard, thus changing your 14" radius. Check the fretboard with your straight edge to make sure it is flat for its entire length. Clean the slots out again. An exacto knife with a #14 blade works great. Stew-Mac has a hook blade for the exacto knife that works very well for that purpose. Any small chips that occur can be glued back, etc.

My fretboards are pre-slotted to .022 wide. If the tang on the fretwire is too big, the neck will develop a reverse bow. This technique is sometimes used on purpose to correct problems with the neck. However, that is not our purpose here. I buy my fret wire from Stew-Mac. It is #148, a medium size. I have found that this is what most players like. Jazz players like a slightly wider wire while others have different preferences. If you are custom building, this is an area that should be decided on before you start. Again, the fret wire tang must not be too tight. By the same token, if it is too loose, frets may pop up and this will affect the playability, sound, etc. The thickness of the tang including the studs (these are what anchors the fretwire) should be about .005 wider than the fret slot for a good fit. See Figure 60.

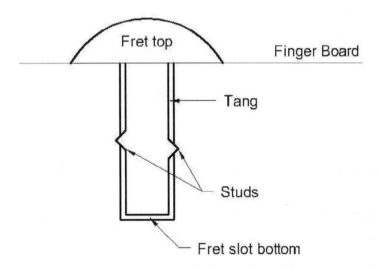

Figure 60 – Fretwire Configuration

The fretwire should be radiused slightly more than the radius of the fretboard. There are tools for this available from several different sources. See the Appendix.

If you buy a coil of fretwire, the radius is just about right. However, this is enough fretwire for several guitars.

Wipe the wire clean with Naptha or laquer thinner as it will have an oil film on it. You can buy a tool that will cut off a section of the tang, leaving the radius top. This will project out over the binding of the fretboard, to be clipped off even and filed when you finish. The tang should reach to the end of the fret slot, minus just a hair. You don't want to break the outer binding loose. See Figure 61.

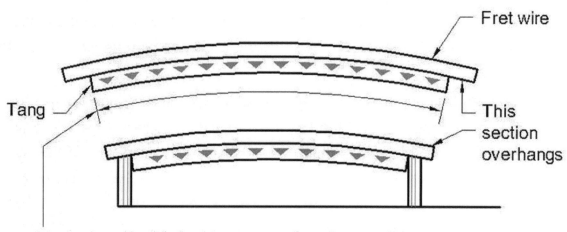

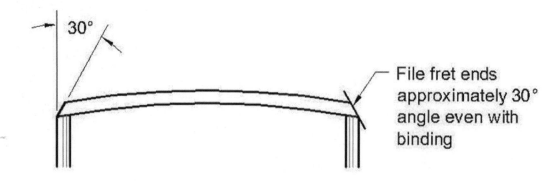

Figure 61 – Fretwire and Trimming

You can also file the tang off, though this takes much longer to do. That is what I did the first few times. If you plan to make many guitars, you will really benefit by the tools that I am mentioning.

Prepare all of the frets before beginning installation. I drilled 23 holes in a block of wood and numbered them, using this as a holder as I prepared them. When you are ready to put them in, start the fret at one end, tap <u>both</u> ends down and then go from the middle to each end. This forces the end area slightly sideways after it is seated, adding to its' gripping power. Use a hard leather or plastic hammer to tap the frets in. A metal one could dent the fret top. Be sure to have a solid block beneath the area you are hammering on and seat the frets solidly. Don't go on hitting the fret after it is seated as this can cause the ends to spring up again. In this case, experience is a great teacher. Any ends that work loose can be glued by putting a drop of thin super glue (the original hot stuff) under the fret and hold it down for a few seconds. See Photo 28.

Photo 28 – Installing Frets

When the frets are all installed, clip the ends even with the binding using flat cutters. Now, using a flat smooth file, file length wise at a 25° - 30°

angle. Be careful not to cut unto the binding or to hit the headstock up by the nut area. See Figure 61 & Photo 32. Final dressing will be done after the neck is installed onto the body of the guitar.

Photo 32 – Trimming Fret Ends

Move on to Chapter 11.

CHAPTER 11

THE NECK – FINAL SHAPING

The first thing you do at this point is to install the fret markers in the fretboard binding. This is done on the base side of the neck to aid the player in seeing fretboard positions while he holds the guitar in the playing position. These should be installed at the same location as your inlays. Just as you used two inlays at the 12th fret, you do the same with the markers. I do mine with 1/16" black plastic rod available from Stew-Mac. Center them top to bottom and between the frets. See Figure 62.

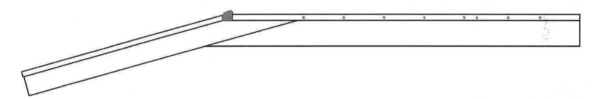

Figure 62 – Fret Markers

After drilling the proper size holes (don't drill too deep, about .060 - .070), use 1 drop of binding cement on top of each hole and push a short piece of rod into the hole. When dry, sand even with the binding.

Now, measure the neck thickness of .820 between the first and second fret and .920 at the 12th fret. Draw a straight line connecting these marks. Do this on each side of the neck. Draw a .900 radius at the heel, leaving the heel thickness at 1/2". See Figure 63.

Figure 63 – Drawing In Neck Thickness

With a grinder, sander, files and rasps, shape the neck. Cut or file the neck even with the binding on each side of the neck. Also, cut the end even. Leave a little material, .030 or so at the cut out area to be final fitted when attaching the neck to the body. See Figure 19.

At this point, you must be pretty confident that you can do this. If not, practice on a scrap piece of wood, a 2" x 4".

I use my belt sander for most of this and use my sight to tell me where I am. I also measure as I go along. Do a little at a time. You don't want to ruin all of the work that you have done up to this point.

You want to leave the neck area under the first fret into the headstock slightly thicker with a tapered contour as in Figure 64.

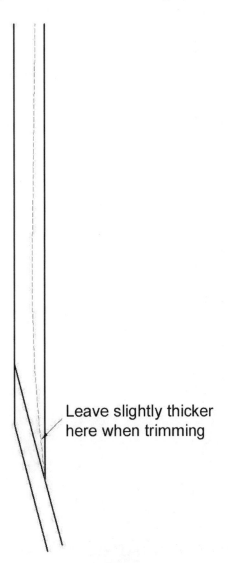

Figure 64 – Thick Area at Head End

This does not interfere with the playability of the guitar while it adds strength where you have already weakened it somewhat with the truss rod access cavity.

You can trace my neck contour shapes onto a piece of poster board or plexiglass and use these as a guide to shaping the neck. Figure 65.

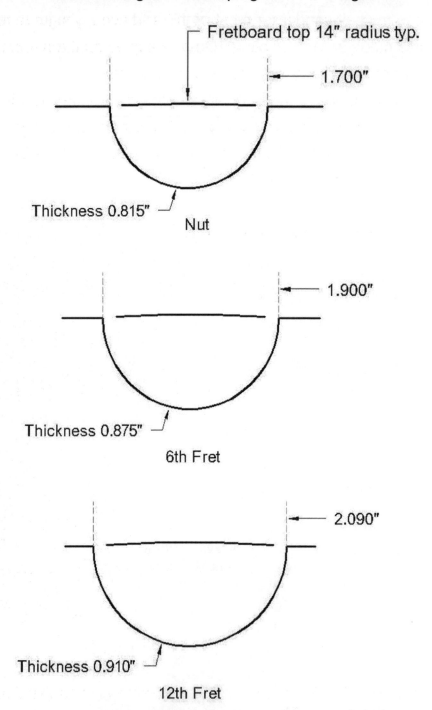

Actual size - To scale

Figure 65 – Neck Contour Shapes

As you get closer to the final shape, go slower. Remember, sanding is going to remove more material. Traditional necks are more rounded than mine are. Again, if you are making this guitar for you, you have more room to experiment. Also, shining lights at different angles on the neck will show you areas that need blending in to make smooth transitions.

When it is time to begin sanding be careful. I use a shoeshine movement on most of the neck. Sight and feel gets the rest done. I hold the neck end in a vise with rubber jaws and support the headstock end with a block while I am shaping and sanding. Photo 29.

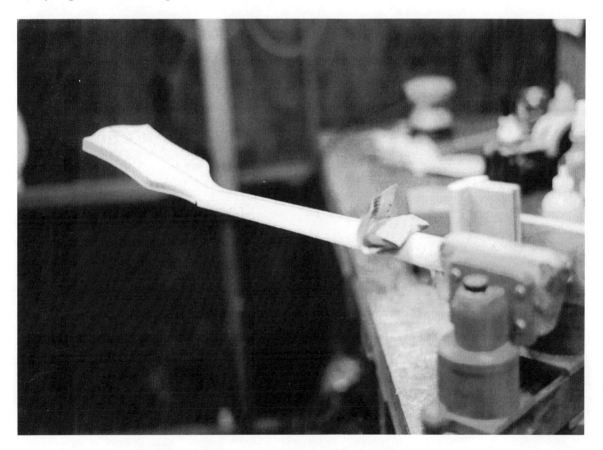

Photo 29 – Shaping and Sanding Neck

Set the neck aside and allow it to normalize for a couple days. You have removed quite a bit of wood and it will change slightly. This is also why you will final size and dress the frets later. We will now deal with the top and binding the 'F' holes and body in preparation for installing the neck.

CHAPTER 12

FITTING THE TOP, CUTTING AND BINDING 'F' HOLES, INSTALLING BRACING

Check your top to be sure that when you clamp it down, you don't have to push more than 1/16" to make it fit flat. We can allow that much because we are using a laminated top and it will easily absorb that much flex without affecting it adversely.

Mark the centerline on both sides of the top. Also mark the center at the top and butt of the body. Holding the top with the center lines lined up, check to see that the peaks of the top and back arches are opposite each other as close as possible. Then holding it in place on the body, mark all the way around leaving 1/8" extra for any final adjustments. Trim to this mark and file the edges smooth.

It is time to cut the F-holes in the top. F-holes have been inherited from the violin family. They can be as individual as the headstock shape, within certain limits. Many of the guitar builders have their own distinct shape and you can tell by the F-hole shape who the builders are. I also have my own design but we will not be doing that shape here, as it is my own design. I will present the more standard type. F-holes can be bound or unbound. Some of the greatest builders have models with unbound F-holes and they look good. The size I will present is designed to have binding installed. An unbound one would be slightly smaller. Size and location are important, as they will affect the sound and the strength of the top. If they are too far apart, this can weaken the top. Also, size affects the tone. Too narrow and the guitar can't breath enough to let the proper amount of air out. Too wide and the guitar won't project as much. True, most of the sound on this guitar will come from the electronics, but a lot of warmth and character also comes from the F holes and the wood which adds to the final sound.

I don't suggest that you experiment in this area too much. Maybe later, after you have built several guitars, you might try changing them a little and develop your own touch. Make a pattern from Figure 65A.

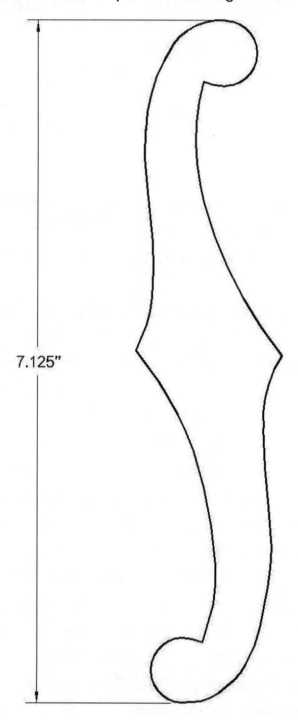

Figure 65a – 'F' Hole Pattern

It can be used for both sides by turning it over. Position them on top as in Figure 66.

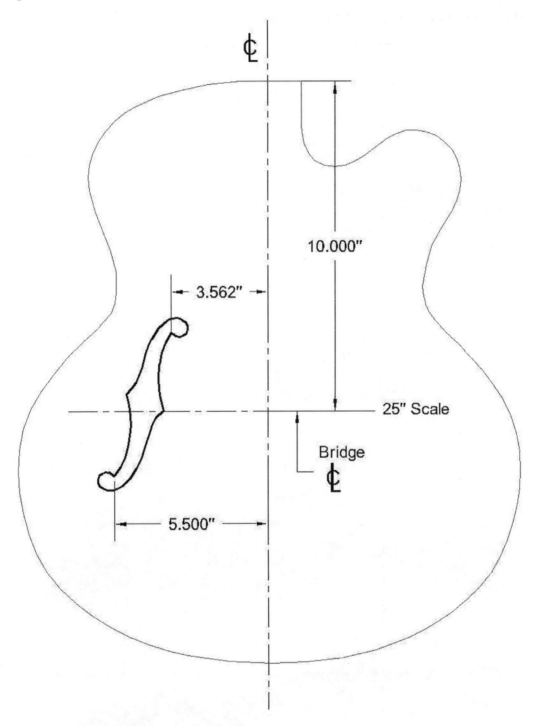

Figure 66 – 'F' Hole Location

Drill a starting hole carefully in each and use a coping saw to cut them out. Clean up the edges with small files and sandpaper on a round dowel. Try to keep your cuts perpendicular to the top, at least as close as you can. Be sure to not chip the top edge as these will show up when you install the binding.

If you have the money and you can find one <u>and</u> you will make many guitars, buy a pin router. See Photo 30, 30a, 30b & 30c.

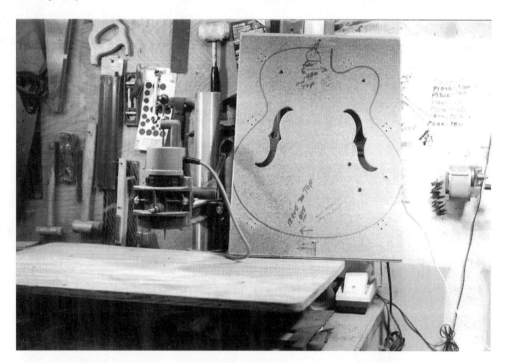

Photo 30 – 'F' Hole Cutting Jig

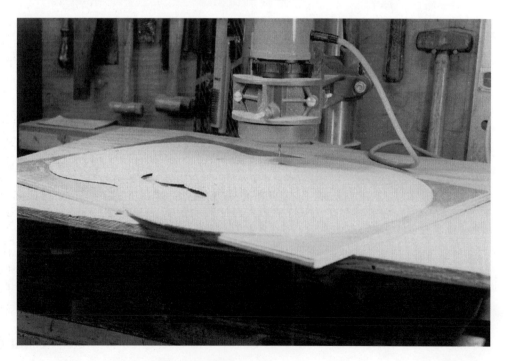

Photo 30a – Pin Router

Jack Block

Photo 30b – Pin Router

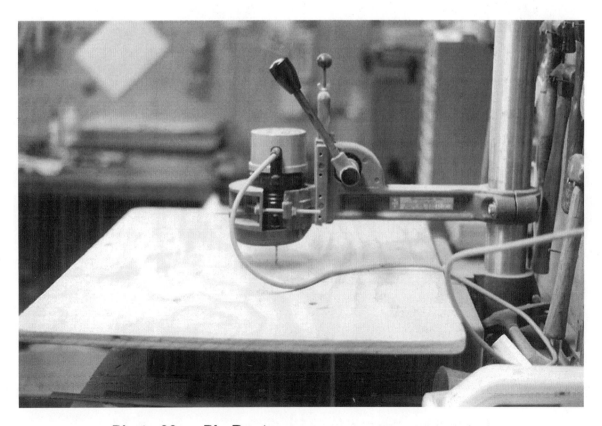

Photo 30c – Pin Router

With a down spiral router bit and a jig to clamp the top onto, this does a beautiful job with very little cleanup required.

At this point, you want to do the binding work as it is much easier when the top is off the guitar. I use a triple binding on my F-holes. It can be installed in one piece making the job much easier. The corners have a mitre on them, as in Figure 67.

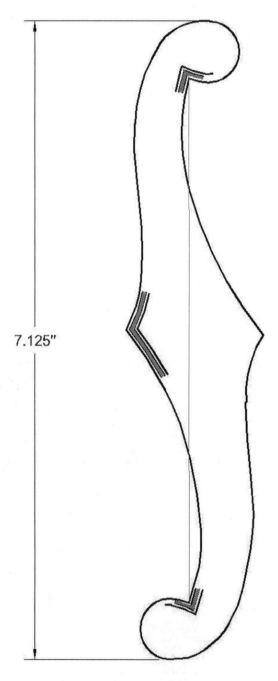

Figure 67 – Mitre 'F' Hole Binding

Bend the pieces in hot water or use a hair dryer as you did when you applied the binding to the headstock. Use strapping tape to hold it in place as before. Remove the tape in about an hour. Let it cure from 24 - 36 hours. If you find any soft spots when you are sanding and scraping, you must let it dry completely. Sometimes this could mean that you applied too much glue.

You are now ready to install the bracing. This has to be done carefully and correctly or the top will not withstand the stress put on it by the bridge and strings. The two types of bracing that are used the most in arch top guitars are parallel and "X" bracing. The sound produced is different. Parallel braces will project better and louder where "X" braces will tend to be softer and more mellow. Since this is primarily an electric guitar, the bracing is not quite as critical to the final sound. It will, however, help strengthen the top, as we are going to cut pick-up holes in the "dome", so to speak. As a result, this is a weakened area and some extra bracing will have to be provided. I learned this lesson first hand and with helpful advice from Bob Benedetto, was able to correct it. Also, my tops and backs and sides are laminated, so we are starting with more strength to begin with.

At this point you must decide on and purchase the pickups that you will use so that you can mark their location. When you install the bracing, you must allow for the pickups. Also, you must decide on your wiring configuration at this point as you will be drilling the pot holes in the top. My controls are a master volume, two pickup volumes, 1 tone control, 1 toggle switch selector, and a jack. See Figure 82 for the layout. Always use a top quality brad point drill bit and a good solid backing so that you don't chip the wood. Use the size you need to fit the threaded shaft on the pot.

Measure down 10" from the top edge of the top. This is the 25" scale length and locates the center of the bridge. Mark this line on the outside and inside of the top. See Figure 66.

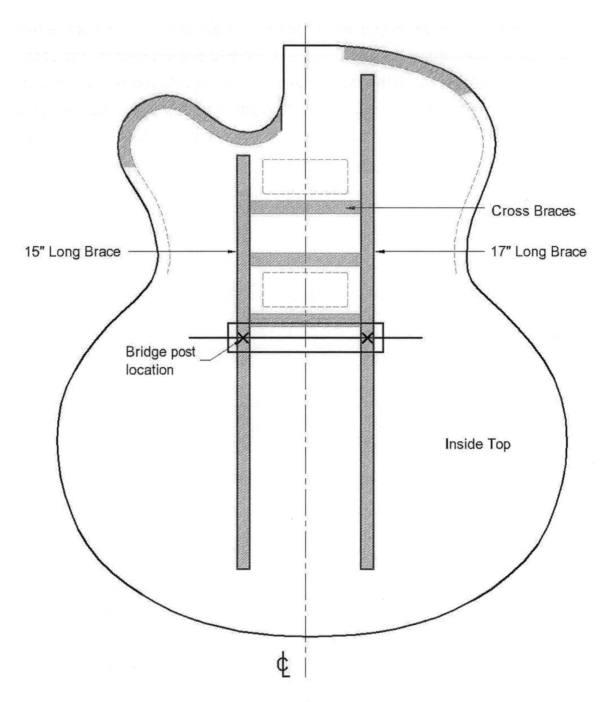

Figure 68 – Bracing Locations

I use a Nashville type bridge with individual string adjustment to allow for correct intonation. The studs are 2.900" apart. This measurement may vary depending on the bridge you use. Space your bracing centers as wide as your bridge studs, leaving room for your pickups in between. This will allow for maximum transmission of sound from the strings to the top of the guitar.

Locate the upper brace ends far enough apart to accommodate the front pickup. The braces are installed in a straight line with these locations. See Figure 68. Also mark the pickup cutout lines on both sides of the top of the guitar. The front pickup edge is 1/4" from the end of the neck and the edge of the bridge pick-up is 1" from the center of the bridge base. See Figure 69.

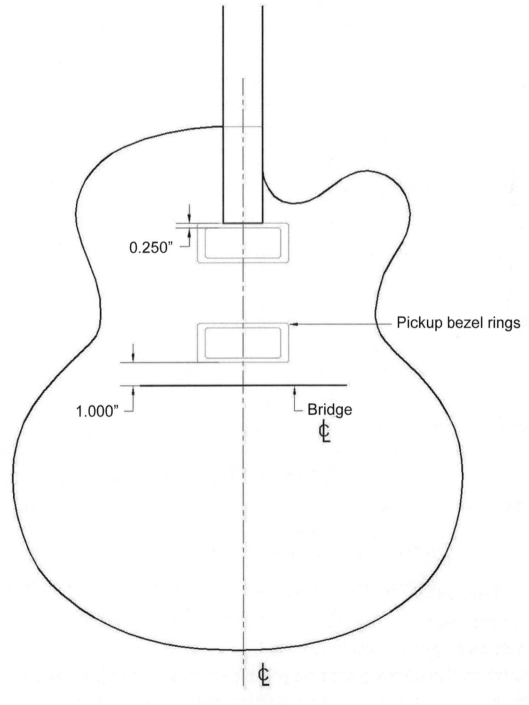

Figure 69 – Locating Pick-Ups

This allows clearance for whatever type of pickup rings you will use. Install the long braces as shown. Also install cross braces as shown to add strength. Otherwise, the top is weak in the areas of the pickup cut outs. See Figures 68 and 69. The front pickup hole location may change according to how many frets you put on your guitar. Some players want the full 24 frets. Instead of, say, 19 or 22. This will move the pickup location, so don't cut any holes in the top until this is determined. At this point, you should have finished the neck anyway, so it shouldn't be a problem. Cut the slot in the top of the guitar where the neck tenon will fit into the headblock slot and mark the end of the fretboard location on the top. That is how you locate the position of the front pickup. Also, you can double check the 25" scale length mark by measuring 25" from the front of the nut slot or the center of the '0' fret while you have the neck in position for marking the front pickup location.

At this point, you are ready to make and install the braces. I use quartersawn spruce. My braces are .312 (5/16") thick by .750 (3/4") high by 15" on the treble side and 17" on the base side. Quartersawn is a must because these give the top most of its missing strength, caused by cutting the pickup and 'F' holes. Lay your top in the mold. Hold the brace in position and using a compass, scribe a line that will duplicate the contour of the top onto the brace. See Photo 31. File or sand to this line. Use carbon paper between the top and brace and by slight movement of the paper the high spots will leave a mark to be sanded, achieving a perfect fit. They must fit exactly, otherwise when clamped they could introduce stresses to the top. See Photo 31a. When you have a perfect fit, apply glue and either clamp or use a weight on top. In one hour, do the other one. Now install the three cross braces at the pickup locations. These must fit exactly to the top and also between the parallel braced. Let all of this dry for 24 hours. The braces must also be as perpendicular to the center plane of the top as possible. See Figure 70 & Photo 31B.

Photo 31 – Scribing the Top Braces

Photo 31a – Clamping and Glueing Braces

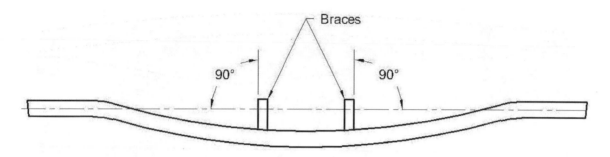

Figure 70 – Braces Perpendicular

Photo 31b – Braces Finished

Using a chisel or grinder, shape the braces. Leave the braces full height for 1" on each side of the 25" scale line and begin to taper them down to 1/8" at each end. See Figure 71 & Photo 31B.

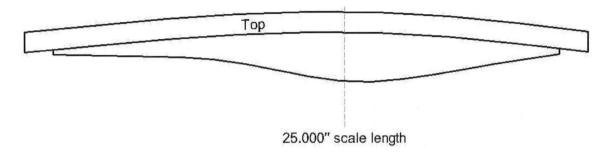

25.000" scale length

Figure 71 – Shaping Braces

This leaves strength where it is needed while allowing the top to move as much as possible. Again, this is not as critical an operation on a laminated top as it would be on a carved top.

Tape 1/2" around the inside on the top and spray 1 or 2 dry coats of lacquer to help seal the wood. This keeps lacquer off of the glueing surface.

Go to Chapter 13.

CHAPTER 13

INSTALLING THE TOP, CUTTING THE PICKUP HOLES, BINDING THE BODY

Before installing the top, check to be sure that the Nec-Loc pin and label have been installed. Also make sure the pot holes have been drilled in the top and the jack hole has been drilled as in Chapter 6.

Apply a small line of glue to the kerfing and spread it evenly. Install the top, matching the centerline marks and clamp with the spool clamps. See Figure 72 and Photo 15.

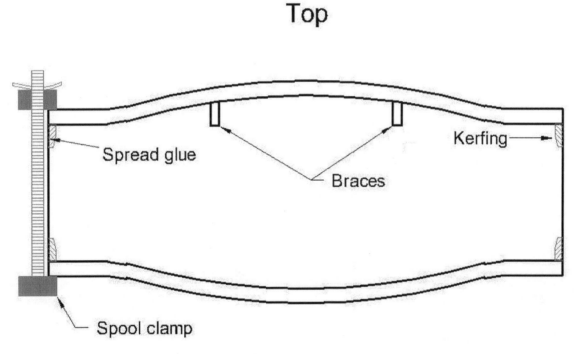

Figure 72 – Glueing Top On

Clean up excess glue and remove the clamps in 1 hour. Let set for 24 hours. Cut the slot in the top at the neckblock in 1¾" to match the mortise on the neck. Sand or file the edges even with the sides. Put the neck in place and check the 25" scale length mark and pickup cutout locations.

Drill a hole at 2 opposite corners of the pickup cutout marks and cut out using a small tapered saw. Clean up the edges. Be sure the cutouts are on centerline and spaced evenly from each other.

Binding grooves can be cut in several ways. Cutting them by hand can be a long and difficult task. They can be done with a dremel tool or a router or even more elaborate techniques. My first was by hand with a violin purfling cutter for a marker then finishing with chisels and files. I do not recommend it! If you have the funds, I suggest you start with a dremel tool set-up. Use the same binding combination of white/black/white that you have throughout. Figure 73.

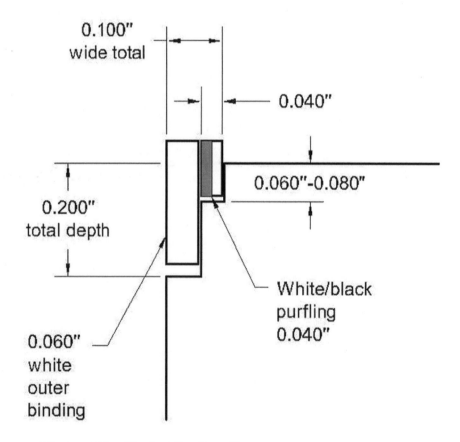

Figure 73 – Body Binding Specs

Stew-Mac sells a dremel set up that will be fine for your first guitar. Make sure the grooves are the right depth and are very clean.

I pre-glue a piece of white/black binding to the white outer binding for a distance of 1" and let it set for 24 hours. Do this to two pieces. Figure 74.

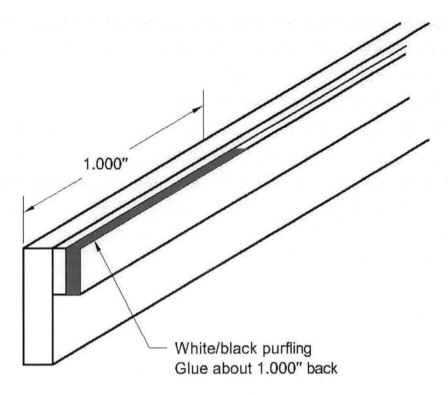

Figure 74 – Pre-Glueing Purfling

This will allow you to mitre the ends on the back of the guitar. See Figure 75.

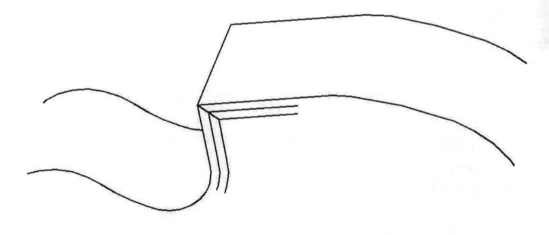

Figure 75 – Mitre Binding On Back

When the fit is perfect, apply binding cement and hold in place with tape. In the small radius areas such as the cut-out and the waist, use strapping tape. The rest can be done with masking tape doubled. Be sure adequate glue is applied on all surfaces, including in the binding grooves. If enough is not applied, it will leave voids between the binding that you can't see. These will show up as indentations in the finish that are hard to fill.

Work your way toward the bottom of the guitar and stop about 4" from the bottom, wiping with a paper towel and taping as you go. Now you can cut and fit the joint at the bottom to get it perfect. The joint on the top will be covered with the tailpiece. Nevertheless, try to get it perfect also. See Figure 76.

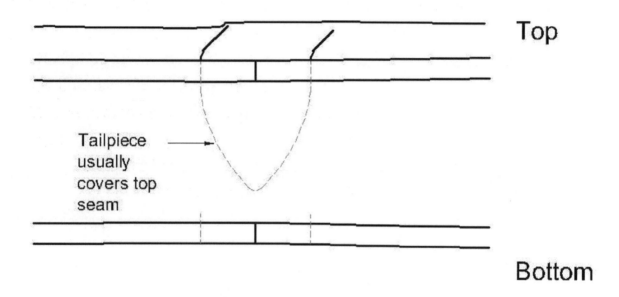

Figure 76 – Bottom Seam On Binding

After 1 hour, remove all tape carefully. This exposes the binding cement to the air and lets it cure. Let set 24 - 36 hours. Scrape even with the guitar body. Slightly round the edges over.

It is easier at this point to sand the body before installing the neck. Start with #100 grit, then go to #220 then to #400. More on this is covered in Chapter 15.

CHAPTER 14

DRILLING TUNER HOLES IN HEADSTOCK, FINISHING THE FRETS, INSTALLIING THE NECK TO THE BODY

At this point, you must decide on and purchase the tuners that you intend to use. There are many different ones on the market. I use the 16:1 ratio Grover Imperials. They require a 3/8" size drill. Use a brad point drill and drill from the top. Any chipping will hopefully be on the back of the headstock and covered with the tuner mechanism. They should be mounted so that the strings don't touch each other when they are wound on the posts. You will have to buy a tapered reamer to final fit the tuners. The headstock is .625 thick. This is ideal for the Imperials, allowing the post to project high enough so that the string has good clearance when wrapped around the post.

If you use the Imperials, follow the dimension in Figure 77.

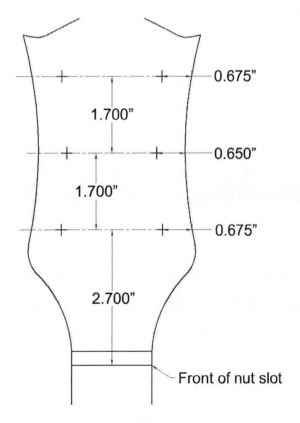

Figure 77 – Tuner Locations

Use a flat block for back-up when drilling the holes. This helps to prevent chipping.

At this point, dress the frets by using either a perfectly flat, smooth file or a 14" radius block 8" long. Use 400 grit on the block and gently go back and forth in a straight line over the fret tops until you can see the sanding mark all the way across all frets.

The frets should now be rounded. The very best tool for this is a diamond file, but they are very expensive. There are less expensive fret files available, like the Gurian fret file. I put masking tape between each fret to protect the fret board surface. Use good light and as you round each top, leave just a hairline mark of the sandpaper. You maintain the fret height that way. Now, use 400 grit to remove all file marks, being careful not to remove any material from the top of the frets. Now go to 600, then I use 0000 steel wool.

Photo 32a – Dressing Fret Tops

If you should use steel wool when the pickups are on the guitar, cover them or they will attract the steel. Also, vacuum often to keep small pieces of steel wool off the guitar. They could work their way into the wood. An alternate method is just to go to 1200 grit, then to 2000 grit without using the steel wool. Now use a small three cornered file with a flat ground on one of the corners. Use this to file up and around the fret ends so they won't cut the fingers when playing. Check first that the frets have been filed at a 25° - 30° angle as in Chapter 10.

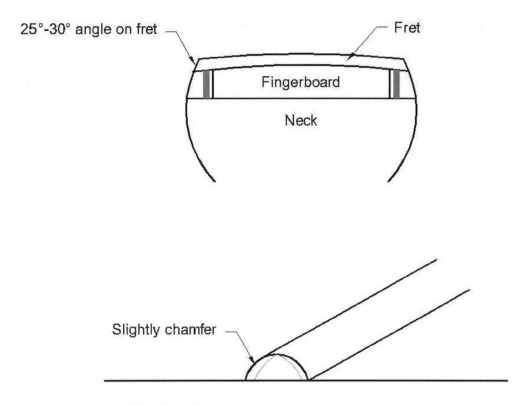

Figure 78 – Fret Dressing

Now, pull all masking tape up and clean everything with Naptha.

Now we are ready to install the neck to the body. This is a very critical step in the whole process. The first thing is to cut out the angle slot in the tenon. This will fit over the nec-loc pin in the headstock mortise, thus locking in the neck. Cut the notch as in Figure 79.

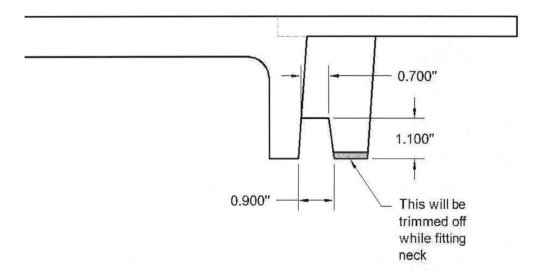

Figure 79 – Nec-Loc Notch

Mark the center line at the top and bottom of the guitar body as in Figure 80.

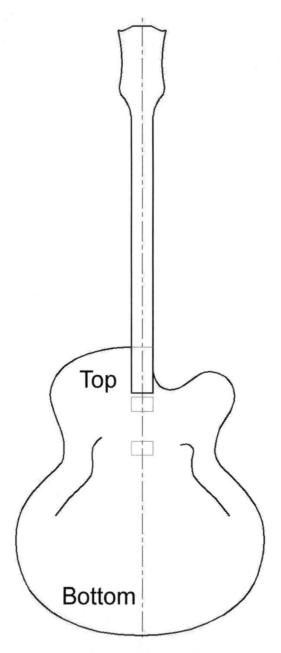

Figure 80 – Everything on Centerline

When the neck is installed, everything should be centered. Check to be sure with a straight edge. This lines up the tailpiece, tuners, etc.

The under side of the neck extension, the part that extends over the body, has to be shaved. Material is taken off until a straight edge over the frets and extending to the 25" scale (the bridge location) has a clearance of .900.

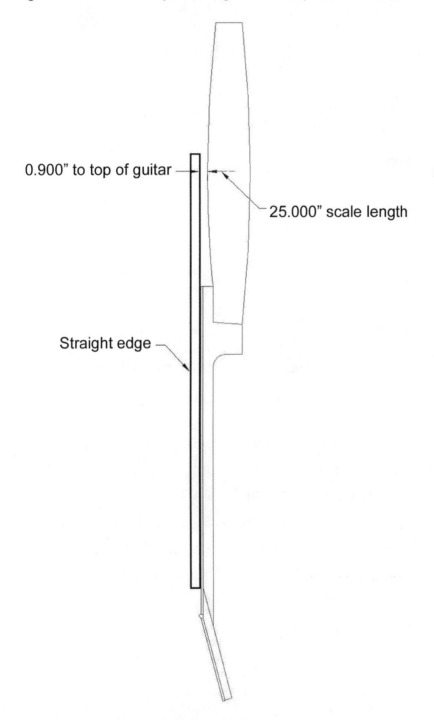

Figure 81 – Straight Edge On Frets

Put the neck in place and using a compass, mark a line following the top contour. The area above the neckblock should touch and the remainder will arch up clear of the top.

Photo 33 – Marking Neck Extension

Using sharp chisels and files, remove the material until you achieve a perfect fit. You may have to take small amounts off of the angle surface where the nec-loc pin makes contact. See Photo 33A. Keep at it until the fit is perfect, using carbon paper between the parts. Slowly pull it out and it will leave marks on the high spots. If you have any real loose spots (because of goofs, etc.) use shims to fill instead of glue. When the fit is right, cut the heel to the right length to accommodate a heel cap. Apply glue to the sides of the mortise and tenon and a small amount to the top of guitar. Put everything together and apply a clamp. See Photo 34

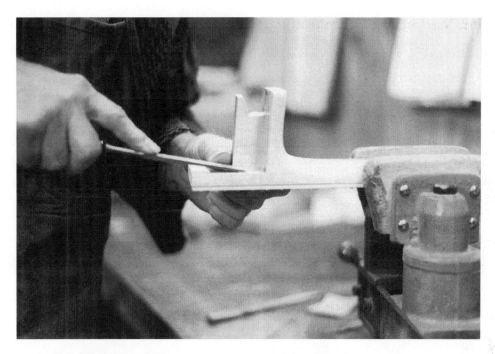

Photo 33a – Trimming Neck Extension

Photo 34 – Glueing Neck On

Use blocks so you don't mark the fretboard or the back of the guitar. It is best to leave it clamped at least twelve hours. File and sand the heel where it contacts the cut out edge until they are even.

Fit and glue up a heel cap, using binding cement if it is plastic.

CHAPTER 15

APPLYING THE FINISH

I will discuss a couple of different methods of putting the finish on the guitar, due to the fact that I live in California. This state has almost regulated the use of nitrocellulose lacquer out of existence. It can still be done in small quantities, but the future is bleak. As a result, you may want to consider the alternative method of using one of the water based lacquers or water base polyurethanes. The advantages are that there is far less damage (if any) to the environment and less damage to your lungs. You also don't smell up the area. Clean-up is with hot water instead of expensive and dangerous lacquer thinners. No thinning is required and they are also non-flammable. A word of caution: you must be sure that the colors you use will be compatible. If you are going to use aniline dyes, the pH must be compatible or you will end up with a gooey glob of crap! I use alcohol based aniline dyes and color tone wood stains.

The three kinds of water based finishes that I have tried are hydro-cote, crystalac, and a polyurethane product made by FSM Corp. and sold by Luthier Merchantile. I find that this product works beautifully, much better than hydro-cote or crystalac.

The two purposes of applying finish to the guitar are to 1) enhance the appearance and 2) to seal the wood, thereby <u>slowing</u> the process of moisture absorption. Absorption will continue, but the finish will help slow it down.

There are many methods out there that will work. Instead of trying to present too many, I will relate what worked for me. That way, you are free to experiment as you want and as your finances will allow.

First, we will discuss nitrocellulose lacquer. It has been used for many years and is considered the traditional finish to apply. There are also polyester lacquers which are mixed in two parts and are chemically cured (similar to epoxy), whereas nitrocellulose cures by evaporation of the solvents. These are known as volatile organic compounds (VOC's) and they are the culprits to the environment, your lungs, etc. Two very important things are a must when using lacquers. First, apply in an area that is well ventilated, as they are extremely flammable. Use caution when pouring to different containers as static electricity can be produced and could ignite vapors. Always have a good fire extinguisher near in more than one location. Secondly, always wear a filter mask designed for the kinds of chemicals that you will be using. Also consider wearing eye protection when you spray. That spray in your eyes is not a very pleasant experience, and can do bad damage to your sight. Later on, if you decide to continue guitarmaking, you should consider building a spray booth.

I have found Lawrence – McFadden clear lacquer to be an excellent finish. This is used by Bob Benadetto - probably the world's leading arched top guitar maker. I read about it in his book and tried it. It works very well. It is available from Luthier Merchantile. It can be brushed on but I recommend spraying it. It does a much better quality job as it can be applied more evenly. Buy a good quality spray gun. Actually, you should buy two guns. One should be a 1qt. size and one, called a "touch up" gun of 8oz. size. Buy the best. If you have to save for a long time, be sure not to use "bargain" guns. After all this work, you don't want to deal with uneven coats, spitting, or runs. It can wipe the smile right off your face and ruin your entire week. Badger makes a good quality "touch up" gun, model 400. Using it with a heavy needle, nozzle and tip, I have sprayed entire guitars with it. It does an excellent job and gives you great control. The 8 oz. container is just right for one good coat of clear lacquer. Learn where the controls have to be set for a dry coat as well as a wet coat, as you will use both. <u>Always</u> practice on scrap wood first before doing the guitar.

As far as colors are concerned, there are so many ways to go that it is almost confusing. To buy them all to experiment with can become very expensive and time consuming. Start with a good standard and later, as time and money permit, you can buy different ones to experiment with. I use colortone wood stains available from Stewart McDonald. They are not quite as colorfast as the aniline dyes, but they mix with almost everything and they are non-grain raising. They can be mixed together to make custom colors.

Now you are ready to check the entire guitar over to make sure everything has been done and you are ready to begin your final preparations for applying the finish. This step is the most important aspect of finishing – the proper preparation of the wood. It must be done correctly or small scratches will show up in the final product, which does not affect the tone or playability of the guitar, but you must try your best to make the guitar as beautiful as possible. People will be looking at your guitar. They may even want you to make one for them. Keep your hands washed clean as you don't want body oils on the wood. This could affect the finish. Begin by sanding the entire guitar with #220 grit Tri – M –Ite that you can buy at auto finishing or hardware stores. Use a sanding block of rubber or thick felt as a backing. Do not sand with your fingers as it will show up as uneven grooves in the finished product. Also, be careful when sanding the face of the headstock if there are inlays. Use a flat hard wood block with the edges beveled for this, as the inlay material sands off at a different rate than the wood. This will leave humps if not done flat. I take my inlays down to 3M 1000 grit. After 220 grit, go to 400 grit. This will remove all 220 grit marks. Always sand in the direction of the grain. Cross grain scratches are difficult to remove and could show up later holding stain. Slightly round the edges of all binding, except for the fretboard. This was already done during its completion.

Now sand all binding with 600 grit to remove all scratches. Using a damp sponge (not too much water) wipe the entire guitar surface. When this dries in about 30 minutes, the wood will feel fuzzy. This has raised the grain. Sand again with 400 grit. If your veneer is not maple but a softer more porous wood, you need to do this operation a second time.

Masking the guitar is next. General purpose masking tape can allow more bleeding under it than the blue Scotch #471 available at auto finishing stores. This stretches and is easier to apply around corners and curves. Doing all the binding makes cleanup for the final clear coats much easier. Use the clear package wrap over the F holes and trim the excess exactly where the binding meets the wood with a razor blade. Clean the residue on the wood caused from the tape with naptha. Mask off the nut slot and the truss rod cut out. Cover the fretboard with masking tape just over the ends of the frets. Use the blue tape on the remainder of the fretboard binding. See Photo 35.

Photo 35 – Guitar Masked Off

Also cover the pickup holes. I install a balloon and blow it up just enough. Now wipe the guitar with Naptha to remove all dust and oils.

After you have practiced on another piece of wood and have achieved the color you want, you are ready to stain the guitar. I use the color-tone non grain – raising stains as I said before. I have found that wiping instead of spraying the stain gives me a much more even color. Wipe the entire guitar and let dry for 1 hour. Have a place to hang the guitar. Use a coat hanger through one of the tuner holes in the headstock, make a loop at the other end and hang it up. See Photo 36.

Photo 36 – Stain and Initial Coats of Finish Applied

Now if there is any porosity in the wood, you can use a good quality sanding sealer. Apply no more than two coats, with 1 hour between coats. Hopefully, your wood won't need to be filled with sanding sealer, as with good quality maple. In that case, you can pull the tape off the binding, clean everything, scrape any color that leaked off onto the binding using a razor blade, and go directly to applying the top coats. This also eliminates the small ledge that the build up of the sealer causes at the binding. If you sprayed sealer, let dry for 24 – 48 hours. Lightly sand smooth with 320 grit. Be very careful not to sand through to the stain and always use felt or rubber backing on your sandpaper to prevent grooves. If any pits remain, a couple more coats of sanding sealer should do it.

Now remove the tape from the F-holes, the body, headstock and fretboard binding. Do this carefully as the lacquer may peel back. Feel along the binding and you will find a small step where the sealer stops and the binding begins. It is impossible to sand this step down even with the binding as you would sand into the stain at the edge. Light, careful sanding with #600 or #1200 grit will remove the sharp edge. If you have not built up the edge too high by applying a lot of sealer, then the remaining ledge will "melt in" with the application of the clear top coats and all but disappear. Using a razor blade or a razor knife, scrape all the stain from the bindings. Clean up the inside surfaces of the F-hole binding also. Be sure the fretboard surface is covered; the nut slot, the truss rod access in the headstock and the pick-up holes should also be covered. You could stuff newspapers in the F-holes but here is another trick. Blow up a small balloon inside the guitar below each F-hole and tie it off. Slip poster board pieces in and the balloons will hold them in place. This keeps the inside clean during this process.

You must apply tape along the fretboard edge just even with the fretwire bottoms so that the binding is exposed and can also be sprayed with the clear coats. When all binding is scraped and sanded clean and the whole guitar is wiped clean with naptha, you are ready to apply the clear top coats.

I thin the lacquer 2 to 1. That is, two parts lacquer and one part thinner by volume. Be sure to use a good grade of lacquer thinner with a medium drying time. Always filter your lacquer. When you are ready to spray, hold the guitar by the neck using a paper towel to prevent body oils from getting on the neck and let the light reflect off the surface so you can see the finish as you apply it. A dry coat will look like dust and a wet coat appears shiny and wet. Spray the body, sides, and head and then carefully hang it with a coat hanger through one of the tuner holes and finish spraying the neck. Spray two coats dry, letting dry 30 minutes between coats. Then spray four coats wet, letting dry 1 hour between coats. Be sure to keep your gun clean by spraying thinner through it between spraying times. Buy a couple extra paint cups for this purpose. Let dry 24 – 48 hours. Lightly sand with #320 or #400 grit. Wipe clean. Spray 3 more wet coats and let dry for one week. When you spray, try to do it in warm, dry conditions.

Wet, cold conditions may necessitate adding retarder to the finish coats in order to prevent orange peel or blushing conditions. You many want to enhance the color by applying a "toner" coat. After applying stain, mix some of your stain with the clear lacquer and spray an even coat or two with the grain to prevent lap marks. When it is dry and the color you like, then proceed with removing the tape and go to the application of the clear top coats.

I guess there are as many methods out there as there are people doing it, but this works well for me. As I said earlier, practice on a similar material then do the guitar. You may find a totally different way than I do, and that is good.

After the guitar has dried for one week, you are ready to break the surface film and allow the lacquer to flash off quicker and dry more complete. The longer it can dry to allow the off gasing of the voc's, the better. With lacquer, when you apply each coat, it "melts" in or "burns" in to previous coats. In effect, spraying X number of coats results in one thick coat.

Use #600 grit wet or dry sandpaper. Start with a bowl of water to which 1 – 2 drops of detergent has been added. Cut your paper into 3" squares and let the sandpaper soak for 30 minutes before using. Dipping the paper in the water to keep it damp, begin sanding in small circular motions. Dip your paper in the water often and clean it with your fingers. This carries away dirt and grit. Sand until no shiny spots appear, just a dull matte finish. Don't forget to use your sanding pads. Use rubber during this phase as felt will absorb too much of the water. Change your water often to keep it clean. Also, wipe the guitar with a clean, damp cloth or paper towel periodically. There is no need to sand the edges too much as they will blend in nicely when buffed. When you are finished sanding the entire guitar, do it again with #1000 or #1200 then wipe it clean and dry it. Photo 37.

Photo 37 – Wet Sanding

Now let the guitar hang for 2 - 3 more weeks to complete the "gassing – off" process. Breaking the surface early in this way speeds up the whole process.

You are now ready to go on to buffing. This can be done several ways. Doing it by hand is a very tedious and time consuming job. The results are okay but using an electric drill with lambswool buffing pad is quicker and will produce a nicer sheen. Start with Meguiar's Glaze #4. When the scratches are gone, go to Glaze #2. Then finish up with Glaze #7. Of course, practice your buffing technique on another piece of material before proceeding to the guitar.

If you can afford it, using a large buffing machine is quicker, easier and does a beautiful job. Stewart McDonald has the buffing wheels and compounds that I use. Use one buffing wheel thickness which is 1" wide for each different compound. This will reach everywhere on the guitar and help prevent heat buildup when using a wheel wider than 1" which could cause a "burn" on the finish. Be very careful as the buffing wheel can catch on the guitar edge, jerk it from your hands, and slam it to the floor. A speed between 800 – 1000 rpm's is ideal. Be sure to buff on the lower half always. See Photo 38.

Photo 38 - Buffer

If the swirl marks weren't removed by your final buff, use a foam pad in an electric drill with Meguiars Glaze #9. This should produce a beautiful shine.

If you will be using crystalac, the process is slightly different. You can use crystalac over the colortone stains but they must be completely dry before applying the "toner" or topcoats. The people at crystalac have designed a coating to go over the stain that helps prevent the clear top coats from penetrating too deeply and putting too much moisture in the wood. Remember, crystalac is approximately 70% water. Also, you do not have to thin it. Use it straight from the can. It looks milky but dries clear and buffs out well.

Recently, I have begun using FSM's product that is available from Luthiers Merchantile. It is a great finish. Water base and non toxic. It is a polyurethane. After staining, if you wish a "toner" coat, mix stain with the material (which looks like milk), apply it then go to the top coats. Also, if your wood is porous, just use several coats of the finish and sand lightly so as not to sand down to the "toner" or stain. Spray 5 – 8 coats with 15 minutes between coats. After 3 days, sand flat with 320 – then spray 3 – 4 more wet coats. Let dry at least one week. Then final sand with #1000 - #1200 grit and buff.

At this point, check over the entire guitar for anything that you may have missed. Feather edge the lacquer on the binding at the fretboard. Remember, you applied tape even with the fretwire bottoms. That leaves a step in this area and must be blended in either using 600 – 1200 grit paper or by lightly scraping with a razor blade. Clean everything, blow out the interior, removing balloons, etc. and you are ready to go to final preparations and assembly.

CHAPTER 16

FINAL ASSEMBLY

This chapter will cover several subjects including installing the electronics, fitting the tuners, installing the truss rod cover, tailpiece, strap buttons, pickguard, fitting and installing the nut and bridge. The next chapter will cover installing the strings and setting up the guitar to play.

The electronics – It is not my purpose here to train you to be an electronics expert. My definition of an "expert" is an "ex" is a has been and a "spert" is a drip under pressure. So don't let anyone call you an expert! Many good sources on techniques and different installations are available from Stewart McDonald.

Gain some background and practice in basic electronic skills before attempting to install them on your guitar. I will cover some basics and some areas where you will need to exercise caution.

There are many different kinds and types of pickups available. Check the source list in the Appendix. I use pickups made by T.V. Jones of Washington on my guitars because that is the sound I want. You may want a different sound. Make sure the pickups you choose will work on your guitar as far as mounting techniques and the heighth at the neck and bridge. I utilize a master volume, a volume for each pickup, a tone control and a toggle selector switch which chooses either pickup separately or both at once. A wide variety of sounds and tones are available from this combination, while not being too overdone in the amount of choices and controls that will be necessary. You may want to try different configurations.

Volume and tone controls are called potentiometers or pots. They come in several types, ie audio taper, linear taper, reverse taper, etc. and many different values measured in ohms such as 100k ohm, 250k ohm, 500k ohm, etc. Pots are basically resistors that can be varied or changed by turning the shaft. A linear taper pot changes resistance evenly whereas an audio taper changes faster at lower levels than at the higher. The linear taper gives a smoother change overall (our ears, however, don't hear this very well) and some people prefer this over the abrupt change that occurs with the audio type. Experimenting will help in your decision. I prefer the audio taper.

Complete Guitar Repair by Hideo Kamimoto and Guitar Electronics for Musicians by Donald Brosnac should give you all the necessary background and skills you need to do an excellent job of wiring your guitar. The following schematic is how my guitars are wired. See Figure 82.

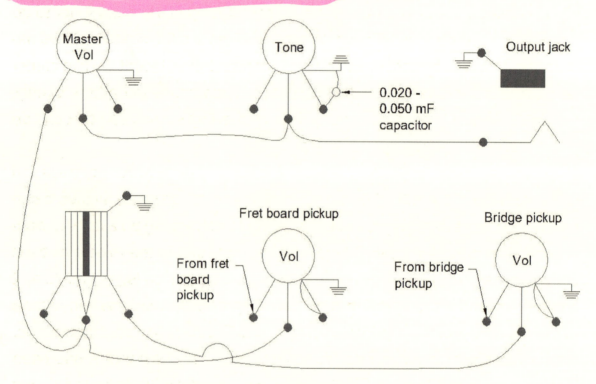

Figure 82 – Electronics Schematics

Make a protective cover for the top of the guitar out of poster board. Cut holes in it where controls go and tape it on the edges in several places. This prevents damage to the top as you work. Use a good quality solder gun and solder for electronics. When you have practiced and can do a good shiny solder joint, you are ready to begin.

Using a cotton swab, wipe a coat of clear lacquer around the inside edges of the holes to help seal against moisture. I use monofilament fishing line to feed down through the holes and bring them out the pickup holes. Tie one end to the pots and pull them up through the hole and fasten them with the washers and nuts. Mine are gold to match all the other gold work on the guitar, available from Allparts. Always use a good quality shielded cable. Bear in mind that you can use different wiring configurations. Experiment to get the sound you want, etc. Also, I use mother of pearl inlaid control knobs to match my inlays (gold) available from L.A. Guitar Works. Electronic components, pots, wiring, etc, are all from Allparts.

Next, fit and mount the tuners. For Grover Imperials, it is necessary to slightly enlarge the holes. I use a hand reamer for this. Be careful not to go too big. The parts should fit snug. When the holes are the right size, seal the insides with a coat of lacquer as you did to the pot holes. Mount the two center tuners first straight out from the headstock. Then space the others evenly. Be careful to use the correct screwdriver for the tiny screws so you don't do damage to the heads.

You are now ready to install the truss rod cover. I make my truss rod cover from the same material as my pickguard, although much thinner. It can be installed in several ways. I use the tiny gold screws, again available from Allparts. You can use 1,2,or 3 screws. I use two, one in the middle of each end. This way, when the truss rod needs adjusting, (which is <u>very</u> seldom) it can be removed without having to remove any strings. If you use two screws at the nut end, you have to loosen the 2nd and 5th strings to get at the screws. Be sure to center it exactly before drilling the holes. Now that it has been located and drilled, leave it off. You may have to adjust the truss rod during final set-up. It is usually the last thing I put on. See Figure 83.

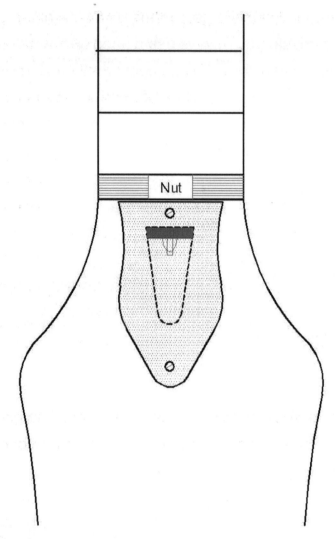

Figure 83 – Truss Rod Cover

    Installing the tailpiece is next. If you should use the Bigsby type, mounting instructions come with each one. They are fairly easy to install. Use a straight edge from the center of the headstock all the way to the bottom of the guitar. Everything should be in line. Mark the center spot. This should be fairly close to where the two pieces of binding meet. I use a piece of heavy fishing line for this, but a long straightedge works fine. When you have established the correct spot, drill the holes and mount the tailpiece. See Photo 39.

Photo 39 – Bigsby Tailpiece

I use metal strap buttons available fro AllParts. One goes in the middle of the tailpiece where it attaches and one goes on the upper bout 1 1/4" – 1 1/2" from the neck edge. See Photo 40 &40A.

Photo 40 – Strap Buttons Installed

Photo 40A – Strap Buttons Installed

The pickguard can be made from many different materials also, but bear in mind that the looks of the guitar should be uniform and pleasing to the eye. If the guitar is trimmed in gold and black, a white pick guard (for example) would be out of place. I make mine from 3/16" – 1/4" Plexiglas. I have my name engraved in reverse in the back and fill the name with black ink. I then apply gold leaf to the back as I did the truss rod cover. I also use the mounting bracket from AllParts as it is very sturdy. Figure 84.

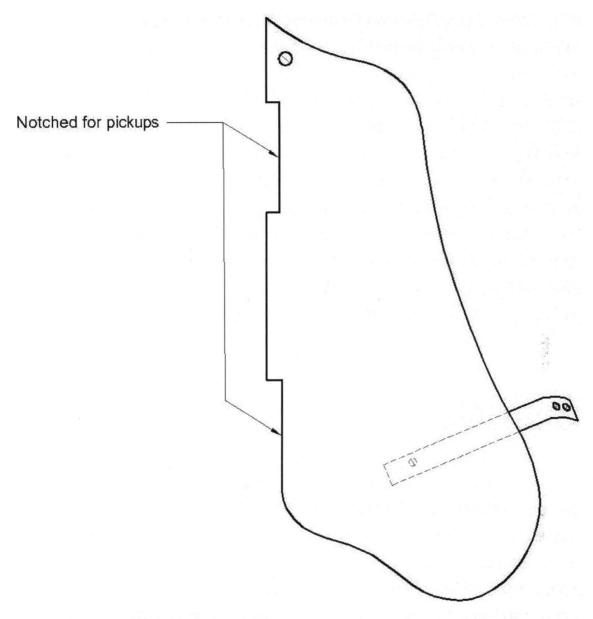

Figure 84 – Pickguard

The nut can be made from many different materials. On my guitars with the vibrato tailpiece, I use the Boron Polytrinate material from Stewart McDonald. This allows the strings to slide easily and stay in tune. On a guitar with a non vibrato type tailpiece, they can be made of bone, plastic, ivory, micarta, steel, brass, almost anything. Bone is preferred by many for good sound. Fitting the nut is somewhat critical for quality reproduction of sound. It is one of the two contact points that the strings make. The other point is the bridge. The notches in both are important as is the fit of the bridge base.

With a good file, clean out the nut slot, being careful to maintain a flat bottom and perpendicular sides. Sand the nut on a flat surface until the fit in the slot is snug. You will be finishing the processing of the nut in the next chapter, set up.

Whether or not you use a complete bridge or make your own base, you must fit the base exactly to the contour of the guitar top. This ensures the best transmission of sound from the strings to the guitar top. I buy the top section from AllParts and make my own base of ebony. Actually, a good time to fit it is after you have finished constructing the guitar and before you apply the finish. Ebony dust can lodge in the pores of the unfinished wood and need to be blown out before sanding. This is easier than re-doing a scratched finish.

Start with a piece of ebony .550 wide by 5.600 long by .450 high. Locate the bridge saddle equidistant from each end and on centerline. Figure 85.

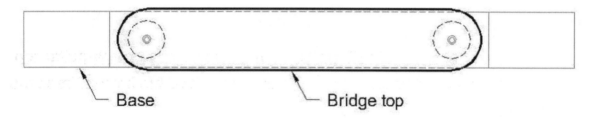

Figure 85 – Bridge Base

Drill the post holes with a #27 drill bit. Drill the holes .185 deep. Holding the saddle in place, thread the studs into the base. See Photo 41.

Photo 41 – Studs Installed in Bridge Base

Now center the bridge base on the 25" scale line on the guitar top. Using a compass as you did when you traced and fitted the braces, trace the top contour onto the base. Photo 42.

Photo 42 – Marking Bridge For Trimming

File or sand to this line. Tape a piece of 80 grit paper grit up centered on the 25" line and sliding the base back and forth, fit it to the top contour until it is perfect. Smooth it with 220 grit. Photo 43.

Photo 43 – Sanding Bridge Base

Now mark a line .550 from the center of each stud and file or grind a 1 1/2" radius on each end, rounding each at the bottom. Figure 86.

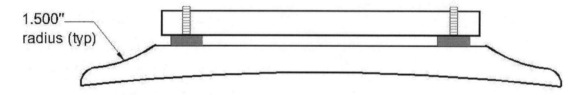

Figure 86 – Radius On Bridge Base

After smoothing to #1200 grit, polish with 0000 steel wool or buff to a shine. I use fretboard finishing oil available from Stew – Mac as a finishing touch. Now assemble your bridge.

CHAPTER 17

SET UP

You have arrived at one of the most critical parts of making a guitar. It is the step that most tells whether or not you have done your work correctly. A guitar that plays well and in tune is a great pleasure and, if you wish to sell your guitar, will do more to help your potential customer make up his mind than all the "Ginger Bread" trimmings that you may have added to the looks. I am reminded of a conversation I had several years ago with Chet Atkins. I was restoring a 1955 Gretsch County Club. I was ready to re-gold plate some of the parts and decided to ask Chet to recommend a good gold plater. He said "Jim, I really don't know any; you know I never really cared how the guitar looked, only that it played right." He was so right! If your guitar does not play right, you might as well put it on your patio and use it as a planter box!

So let's make the guitar play as it should. First, check the neck with your straight edge to see if it has changed. Make sure the frets are level as you did in Chapter 14.

Use a straight edge to span just three frets at a time. If it rocks back and forth, the center fret is high. Start at the nut and check for high frets, adjusting them as you go with #400 grit paper. Now, your fretboard should be very near perfect. You might have to do this several times.

Now you are set to final shape the nut and file the string notches on the nut and bridge. Make sure the string spacing is correct. Start with a set of medium strings. There are many theories out there on this subject and I won't cover them all here. You are left to research this at a future date if you so desire. You need to buy a set of nut files at this point. They will make the most accurate slots. This step is critical. If done incorrectly, you will chase buzzes and noises for days. Also, you won't achieve the best sound. The energy that is transferred to the guitar body and electronics is created between the contact points of the nut and the bridge when the strings are strummed or plucked. If the contact points are not correct, then you lose some of that energy, which will affect your sound. These files are available from Stewart McDonald at a nominal cost. An X-Acto saw blade #378 is .013". It is good for the small E string. From there, try to buy files that will give a groove from .003" to .005" wider than the string.

     Basically, you space the strings evenly, either by eye or measurement. I begin by installing the first and sixth string loosely. Set the bridge at 25" from the front of the nut slot. If a '0' fret design, then measure from the top center of the '0' fret. Some people like the base strings spaced wider than the treble strings and some like it just the opposite. If you are making this guitar for a specific person, then you do it as that person wants. If the guitar is for sale, then you go down the middle path and if the person who might buy it wants to change it, he or she is free to do so. Lay the first string on the nut and the bridge saddle in from the end of the frets so that if it is pulled or bent, it won't fall off the edge easily. Mark the nut and bridge saddle. Do the same with the sixth string. These should be about the same distance in from the edge on a steel string electric. Again, some prefer one or both either in more or closer to the edge. I put mine slightly more than 1/8" in, approximately .150". Notch the bridge saddle just enough to hold the string in place and return to the nut. Shape the nut as in Figure 87.

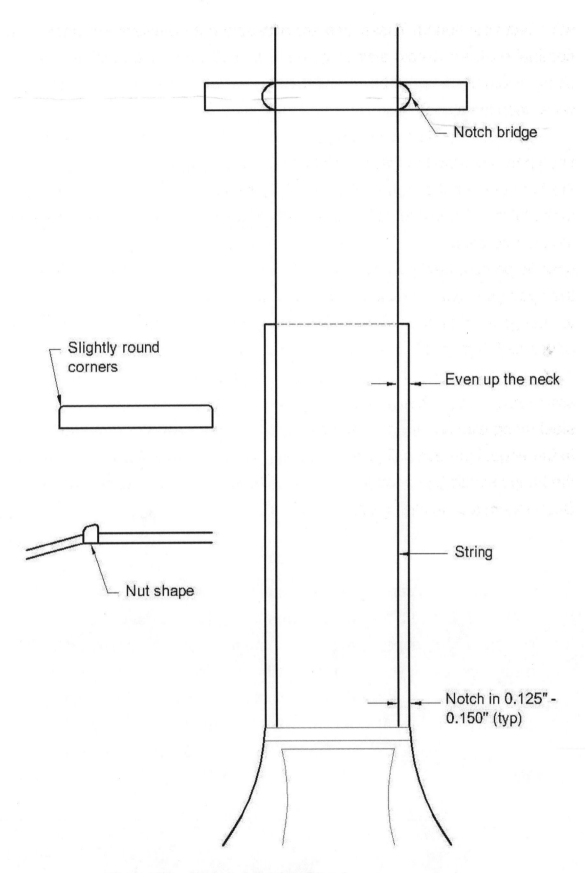

Figure 87 – Nut and Bridge Shaping

When the string passes over the nut, it should make contact with the full surface of the nut, coming solid off the front, not only to maintain the correct scale length but also for the cleanest and best sound. The same thing is true of the bridge saddles. When you make the slots, slant them as in Figure 88.

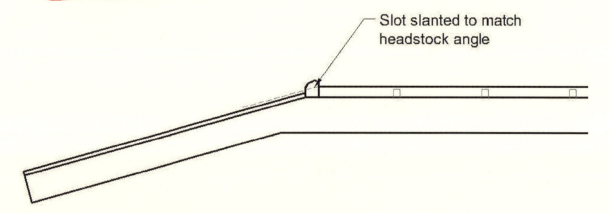

Figure 88 – Slanting String Slots

Make the nut slot just deep enough so that when the string is pushed down at the second fret, it clears the first fret by about .005". A good set of feeler gages is a good way to check this. If the string touches the first fret at this point, it can cause buzzing. Do the same with the sixth string, only it should clear the first fret by .010" or so. The strings should clear the first fret slightly more as you go from the first to the sixth string. Don't forget to file on a slant with the headstock. Also, open the rear of the slots slightly more than the front so the string can angle toward the tuner post without buzzing on the rear of the slot. Leave a few thousandths to be cleaned out of the bottom of the slots with 1200-grit paper to make a smooth bottom for the string to slide on. This is important if you are using a vibrato tailpiece.

Now slot the bridge saddles just a little more at this point so the strings are held firmly in place. At this point, install the rest of the strings, bending each string back on itself as per Figure 89, making a non-slip anchor on the tuner post.

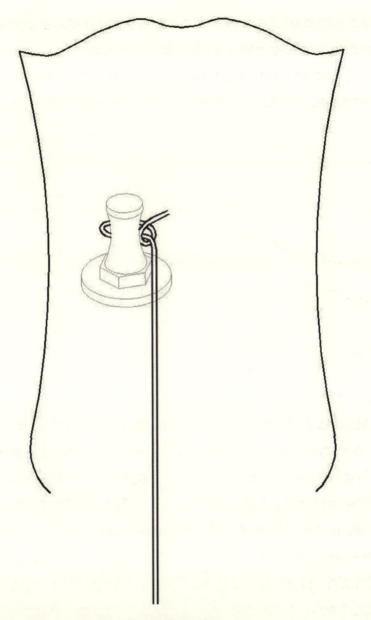

Figure 89 – Installing Strings On Post

Leave enough string to make 2 - 3 windings on the posts. Slot the nut in a similar manner for each string as you did for the first and sixth string. Either measure to the centerline of each string or use your eye for proper spacing. Proceeding to the bridge, space and notch as you did to the nut with this difference. The radius that the string bottoms make across the end of the fret board should be slightly larger than the radius of the fretboard. If your fretboard is 14"R then the strings should be 15", etc. Make a 15" gage and using it at the bridge, notch accordingly. Refer to Figure 90.

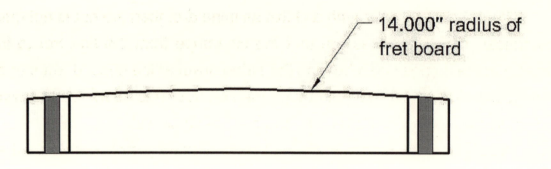

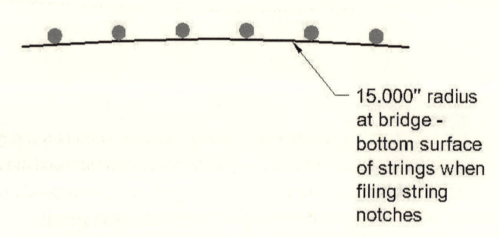

Figure 90 – Radius at Fretboard and Bridge

Now file the top of the nut down as in Figure 87. You want to leave enough material so the strings won't come out of the slots during heavy picking or bending. Sand the ends even with the neck edge and slightly slant the top as in Figure 87. Finish sand with #600 grit being sure not to sand too much off the sides. It should still fit snug.

Buff it up and install with 1 drop of white glue. This will hold it firmly in place, while also making it easy to remove in the future. White glue releases with the application of very little heat as compared to other kinds of adhesives. Now bring the strings up to pitch. Be careful here as I have had strings break and hit me in the face. There is approximately 120 - 150 pounds of force now pulling on the neck from the strings. That is quite enough to put an eye out, so I suggest that during this operation, you use safety glasses.

If your guitar is built with a O fret as mine are, then the nut is not quite so critical. The differences are that the clearance from the first fret to the bottom of the strings when holding the string down at the second fret can be reduced to O. That is, they can touch the first fret. This allows a little lower action setting. Also, the slots in the nut are not so critical.

Your next step is to adjust the truss rod for proper clearances. When a string is plucked, it vibrates around a complete circular path. The point of maximum deflection is at the center of its length as in Figure 91.

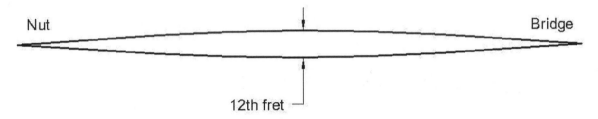

Figure 91 – Plucked String Path

According to Mr. Kamimoto of Kamimoto Strings (who has a physics backgound), this deflection is more in a parabolic configuration and the relief I use is based on his chart. There is a very complete and thorough chart and is available for anyone to study in his book, <u>Electric Guitar Set-ups</u>.

If the neck has no relief, then the vibrating string will hit the frets, causing a buzz. The pull of the strings on the neck causes it to bow or bend as in Figure 92.

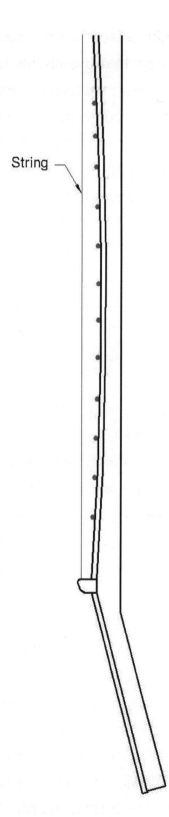

Figure 92 – Neck Bow Under Tension

This will change with the gauge of strings used. Light strings don't bow it as much as heavy strings. Light strings also vibrate in a larger arc, thereby requiring more relief and a higher action. Lay your straight edge between the front edge of the nut or '0' fret and the twelfth fret. Using a light to see between it and the fret tops, check for clearances as per Figure 92.

Do this while holding the guitar in the playing position and tuned to correct pitch. Just the weight of the neck can change the amount of relief present by several thousandths. The amount of relief depends on the action you want at the twelfth fret. Action is the height of the string above the fret, measured from the top of the fret to the bottom edge of the string. If the action at the twelfth fret is 4/64 (1/16 or.0625"), then the relief should be .004" at the 1st fret, .008" at the 2nd fret, .010" at the 3rd, .012 at the 4th, .013 at the 5th, 6th, and 7th, .012 at the 8th, .010 at the 9th, .007 at the 10th, and .004 at the 11th. These figures are taken from Mr. Kamimoto's book, page 78. You can see from his chart that the amount of relief required is not the same on each side of the 6th fret. This is also the ideal perfect situation, seldom if ever achieved. Lighter strings (vibrating in a larger arc) will require more relief and also a higher action as stated earlier. The truss rod should require very little movement to make a change. One quarter of a turn at a time is adequate. Tightening the rod removes relief while loosening it lets the neck bow more. This setting will change as the neck settles in. Sometimes this can take several months. If there is no change by the time you have turned the adjusting nut ½ turn, stop because something is wrong and over tightening can result in a broken rod.

Ideally, relief is measured between the nut and the 12th fret. From the 12th fret to the 16th fret or so, the frets should be level and after the 16th fret, there should be some slight fall away (slightly more clearance at each fret as you progress to the end of the fret board). This will provide the most perfect playing condition and will allow the lowest action possible.

Now proceed to the bridge and adjust it up or down for the action height that you prefer. I usually adjust it downward as far as possible until buzzing occurs. Then raise it just until the buzzing stops. You should now have a very easy playing neck.

At this point, you set the intonation. This can be done by ear but the best way is to invest $20 or so in an electronic tuner. The reason you must set the intonation is so that each string will be as accurate as it can be, when fretted within the confines of the equal tempered tuning system. The theory and mechanics of this system are thoroughly explained in <u>Complete Guitar Repair</u> by Hideo Kamimoto. Adding the right amount of compensation to the scale length of the string, which in our case is 25", sets intonation. The string is set at a certain height above the frets, reflecting the particular style of the player and also to eliminate buzz. When the string is pushed down to the fret, it is stretched, making it go sharp. This sharpness increases as you move up the neck because the string height above the fret is higher as you move in that direction. This sharpness, which must be corrected for, is the reason for intonation adjustment. It is done by moving the string saddle at the bridge backwards or forwards. Start with all the strings tuned to the correct pitch. Now note the harmonic of the string at the twelfth fret. Now play the fretted note at the same fret. If the fretted note is higher than the harmonic, then the string is playing sharp and the saddle has to be adjusted away from the fingerboard. If it is flatter then the harmonic, it must be moved toward the fingerboard. The two notes must match exactly.

The final adjustment in your set-up process is to adjust the pick-ups. Different pickups do different things and there are dozens of different ones out there. I use

pickups made for me by T.V. Jones in Washington, He can give you any sound you want. Also, he can make a Gretsch looking pickup sound like a Gibson or vice versa. The fretboard pick up should be between 1/16" to 1/8" below the string when fretted at the highest fret. More powerful pickups can adversely affect the sound if they are closer than this. More powerful magnets can pull on the string too strongly. Adjust the screws accordingly for string to string balance as well as balance between the two pickups for volume. I use my ear for the most pleasing balance but this can also be done with meters. In the end, your ear is probably the best indicator.

Now your basic set-up is complete. Do it again. The whole thing. You will make some slight changes that may surprise you. Remember that string gauges, action height, playing styles, preferences, all of these and more could affect the settings. Light strings = higher action = intonation changes = pickup adjustment changes etc., and vice-versa.

APPENDIX

Supplies & Tools

Allparts
13027 Brittmorre Park Dr.
Houston, TX 77041
1-800-327-8942
www.allparts.com
all parts and supplies

Ameritage Carrying Cases
540 E. Centralia St.
Elkhorn, WI 53121
1-800-315-3051
www.ameritage.com
cases

Cascade Tools, Inc.
P.O. Box 3110
Bellingham, WA 98227
1-800-235-0272
tools and supplies

Certainly Wood Veneers
11753 Big Tree Rd., Rt. 20A
Aurora, NY 14052
1-716-655-0206
www.certainlywood.com
veneer

Chandler Guitars
370 Lang Rd.
Burlingame, CA 94010
1-415-342-1490
www.chandler-usa.com
supplies and instruments

Constantines
2050 E. Chester Rd.
Bronx, NY 10461
might be in florida now?
some wood and veneers

Custom Pearl Inlay
Route 1, P.O. Box 240
Low Road
Malone, NY 12985
1-518-483-7685
www.valleygrass.ca/cpinlay.html
pearl inlay and supplies

D&F Products
6735 Hidden Hills Rd.
Cincinnati, OH 45230
1-513-232-4972
Gretsch parts

Davitt Hanser
4940 Delhi Pike
Cincinnati, OH 45238
1-800-451-4944
www.sayhhi.com
musical instruments and supplies

Duke of Pearl
18072 Greenhorn Rd.
Grass Valley, CA 95945
1-916-273-4116
pearl inlay and supplies

Elderly Instruments
1100 N. Washington Ave.
Lansing, MI 48901
1-517-372-7890
www.elderly.com
music instruments and supplies

Enco Manufacturing
5000 W. Bloomingdale Ave.
Chicago, IL 60639
1-800-873-3626
www.use-enco.com
tools and supplies

Euphonon Co.
P.O. Box 100A
Orford, NH 03777
1-603-353-4882
guitar maker supplies

Exotic Woods, Co.
444 Chews Landing Rd.
P.O. Box 532
Sicklerville, NJ 08081
1-800-GIDWANI
www.exoticwoods.com
all woods for builders

Ferree's Tools, Inc.
1477 E. Michigan Ave.
Battle Creek, MI 49014
1-800-253-2261
www.ferreestools.com
repair tools and supplies

Fritz Kollitz Fine Tonewood
Kairlindacher Strasse 2 D-91085 WEISENDORF
Germany
0049-9135-2804
www.kollitz.de
tone woods

Grizzly Imports, Inc.
P.O. Box 2069
Bellingham, WA 98227
1-800-541-5537
machinery, tools, vac supplies

The Guitar Makers Connection
(division of C.F. Martin Co.)
P.O. Box 329
Nazareth, PA 18064
1-800-247-6931
wood and tools

Harbor Freight Tools
3491 Mission Oaks Blvd.
Camarillo, CA 93010
1-800-423-2567
www.harborfreight.com
tools and supplies

Harptone Manufacturing
1013 Broadway
Brooklyn, NY 11221
1-800-535-5563
cases

Hartville Tool
13163 Market Ave. N
Hartville, OH 44632
1-800-345-2396
www.hartvilletool.com
tools

Industrial Abrasives
642 N. 8th St.
P.O. Box 14955
Reading, PA 19612-9954
1-800-428-2222
www.industrialabrasives.com
sanding supplies

International Luthiers Supply, Inc.
P.O. Box 580397
Tulsa, OK 74158
1-918-835-4181
www.internationalluthiers.com
supplies for making and repair

International Violin Company, Ltd.
1421 Clarkview Rd., Ste. 118
Baltimore, MD 21209
1-800-542-3538
www.internationalviolin.com
tools and supplies

Jones-Fletcher Music Co. Inc.
P.O. Box 756
South Yarmouth, MA 02664
1-800-325-3221
cases

Klingspors' Woodworking Shop
856 21st St Dr. SE
P.O. Box 3737
Hickory, NC 28603-3737
1-800-228-0000
www.woodworkingshop.com
sanding supplies

L.A. Guitar Works
19320 Vanowen St.
Reseda, CA 91335
1-818-758-8787
pearl inlay knobs

Lee Valley and Veritas
P.O. Box 1780
Ogdensburg, NY 13669-6780
1-800-871-8158
www.leevalley.com
tools

Leichtung Inc.
4944 Commerce Pkwy.
Cleveland, OH 44128
1-800-321-6840
tools and supplies

Luthiers Merchantile International
P.O. Box 774
412 Moore Ln.
Healdsburg, CA 95448
1-800-477-4437
www.lmii.com
wood, parts, and supplies

MSC Industrial Direct Co., Inc.
75 Maxess Rd.
Melville, NY 11747-3151
1-800-645-7270
www.mscdirect.com
tools

Micro Mark
340 Snyder Ave.
Berkeley Heights, NJ 07922-1595
1-800-225-1066
www.micromark.com
small tool specialists

Musicorp
P.O. Box 30819
Charleston, SC 29417
1-800-845-1922
www.mbtinternational.com
musical instruments and supplies

Northern Tool & Equipment
P.O. Box 1499
Burnsville, MN 55337-0499
1-800-533-5545
www.northern-online.com
tools

Old World Art
1953 S. Lake Pl.
Ontario, CA 91761
1-909-947-4928
www.caldexcrafts.com
gold leaf supplies

Reliable Buff Company
226 Bivens Rd.
P.O. Box 942
Monroe, NC 28110
1-704-289-4300
www.reliablebuff.com
buffing wheels

Ridge Carbide Tool Corp.
585 New York Ave.
P.O. Box 497
Lyndhurst, NJ 07071
1-800-443-0992
www.ridgecarbidetool.com
router supplies

Rockler Woodworking & Hardware
4365 Willow Dr.
Medina, MN 55340
1-800-279-4441
www.rockler.com
tools

Stewart McDonald
21 N. Shaffer St.
P.O. Box 900
Athens, OH 45701
1-800-848-2273
www.stewmac.com
all supplies for builders

T.V. Jones
P.O. Box 2802
Poulsbo, WA 98370
1-360-779-4002
www.tvjones.com
custom pick-ups

Trend-Lines Inc.
P.O. Box 6447
Chelsea, MA 02150
1-800-767-9999
tools and supplies

Tru-Grit
760 E. Francis St., #N
Ontario, CA 91761
1-909-923-4116
www.trugrit.com
sanding belts

WD Music Products Inc.
4070 Mayflower Rd.
Fort Myers, FL 33916
1- 941-337-7575
www.wdmusicproducts.com
supplies

Willard Brothers Woodcutters
300 Basin Rd.
Trenton, NJ 08619-2046
1-800-320-6519
www.willardbrothers.net
wood supplies

Woodcraft Supply
41 Atlantic Ave.
Woburn, MA 01888
1-800-225-1153
www.shop.woodcraft.com/woodcraft
tools and supplies

Woodhaven
501 W. 1st Ave.
Durant, IA 52747-9729
1-800-344-6657
www.woodhaven.com
tools

The Woodworkers Store
21801 Industrial Blvd.
Rogers, MN 55374
1-800-279-4441
tools and supplies

Woodworkers Supply
5604 Alameda NE
Albuquerque, NM 87113
1-800-645-9292
www.woodworker.com
tools and supplies

X-Acto
1-800-873-4868
www.hunt-corp.com
exaction knives and supplies

Luthier Organizations

ASIA
(Association of Stringed
Instrument Artisans)
Editor – Rick Davis
1394 Stage Rd.
Richmond, VT 05477
1-802-434-5657

GAL
(Guild of American Luthiers)
8222 S. Park Ave.
Tacoma, WA 98408-5226
1-253-472-7853
www.luth.org

Players Organizations

AFG
(Association of Fingerstyle Guitarists)
2457 Vista del Monte Dr.
Acton, CA 93510
New address on web site –
P.O. Box 761
Anaheim, CA 92815-0761
1-661-269-4556
www.afg.org

CAAS
(Chet Akins Appreciation Society)
3716 Timberlake Rd.
Knoxville, TN 37920

Annetta & Richard Glick
Fine Guitar Consultants –
Special Consultation and Representation
1-619-265-5900
www.fineguitarconsultants.com

INDEX

A

Abrasives 161
adjust 63, 137, 151, 153, 154
adjustment 63, 72, 106, 154, 155
angle 54, 57, 61, 68, 81, 92, 118, 119, 122, 148
aniline 125, 126
applying 12, 125, 127, 129, 130, 131, 134
Archtop Guitar xiii, 73
audio 135

B

back x, 3–5, 7, 9, 10, 12, 18, 25, 26, 30, 32, 35, 37–41, 47, 57, 69, 71, 77, 81, 89, 99, 115, 117, 118, 123, 130, 140, 144, 145, 148, 173
bending 8, 23, 25, 26, 27, 148, 150
Bending Iron 8, 23, 25, 26, 27
binding 40, 74, 77, 78, 82, 83, 85, 86–92, 97, 99, 102–104, 114, 115, 116, 123, 127–130, 134, 138
blocks 83, 123
body xiii, xix, 3, 8, 13, 15, 31, 32, 35, 37, 40–42, 49, 50, 51, 57, 80, 82, 85, 92, 94, 97, 99, 116, 119, 120, 121, 127, 130, 145
Braces 105, 110, 111, 143
bridge 6, 9, 37, 105, 106, 107, 121, 135, 141, 142, 143, 144–148, 153, 154, 174
bridge base 6, 107, 141, 143
buffing 132, 164
building xvii, xxvii, 1, 89, 126

C

Cases 8, 157, 161
cement 77, 93, 115, 116, 123
Chips 77, 89
cleaner 1, 54
clearance 18, 108, 117, 121, 151, 153
colors 80, 125, 126, 173
construction xiii, xvii, xviii, 3–6, 51
cover iv, x, xix, 50, 71, 118, 128, 135, 136, 137, 140, 145, 173
cutter 114

D

dots 77
Drawing xiii, 7, 13, 16, 94
dyes 125, 126

E

Ebony xviii, 6, 54, 59, 61, 71, 73, 79, 80, 142, 173, 174
End Grain 3, 4, 32, 35
epoxy 8, 9, 72, 77, 89, 125
Equal Tempered Tuning 73, 154
equipment 1

F

filling 11
fitting 27, 135
fret 8, 32, 57, 62, 65, 68, 73, 73–77, 77, 83, 88–93, 89, 91, 93, 97, 108, 118, 121, 128, 145, 145–149, 146, 151, 153, 154
fretboard xix, 6, 63, 73–77, 78, 82, 83, 86–89, 88, 93, 108, 118, 123, 127–130, 134, 144, 145, 149, 153, 154, 173
F holes 99, 127

G

glueing 13, 28, 40, 49, 51, 54, 60, 61, 77, 80, 111
Gretsch xxviii, 145, 154, 158
Grover Imperials 117, 137

H

head 3, 31, 33, 35, 57, 62, 71, 130
heel cap 122, 123
humidity 1, 4

I

Inlay 26, 77, 80, 83, 127, 158, 159, 162
installation 91
installing 40, 80, 82, 97, 113, 116, 135, 146

J

jack 47, 105, 113

K

kiln dried 6

L

lacquer 12, 50, 111, 125, 126, 130–132, 134, 136, 137
Lawrence – McFadden 126
Les Paul xvii
linear 135
Lutherie xvii, xxvii

M

making ix, xiii, xvii, xviii, xxvii, 1, 3, 7–9, 25, 26, 40, 73, 97, 104, 145, 146, 148, 150, 154, 161
maple 3–5, 7, 11, 25–27, 30, 31, 36, 44, 51, 59, 62, 71, 73, 127, 129, 173
masking 8, 85, 115, 118, 119, 127
material 4, 6, 8, 31, 38, 48, 51, 73, 77, 80, 94, 97, 118, 122, 127, 131–133, 137, 141, 150
material for 8
measuring 108
metal 91, 139
mounting 135, 138, 140

N

Naptha 90, 119, 128, 130
neck xv, 3, 5, 8, 11, 32, 33, 37, 44, 50, 51, 54–56, 57–59, 61–63, 68–77, 81, 85, 89, 92–97, 107, 108, 113, 116, 119, 121, 122, 130, 135, 139, 145, 150–153, 173

nitrocellulose lacquer 125
non-grain raising 126
nut 62–64, 68–70, 74, 81, 82, 83, 85, 86, 92, 108, 127, 130, 135, 137, 141, 142, 145–149, 153

O

orange peel 131

P

paper 8, 22, 26, 27, 61, 75, 108, 116, 122, 130, 131, 134, 144, 145, 148
Pearl xxvii, 73, 77, 80, 137, 158, 159, 162, 174
Pick-Ups 107, 154, 165
pickguard 44, 45, 135, 137, 140, 174
placement xviii
potentiometers 135
pots 135, 136
preparation 7, 49, 97, 127

Q

Quartersawn 3, 4, 5, 6, 31, 36, 51, 59, 73, 108

R

radius 75, 77, 78, 89, 90, 93, 115, 118, 144, 149
relief 151, 153
Rosewood 6, 73

S

safety 1, 150
sanding 5, 11, 12, 15, 25, 27, 41, 54, 62, 75, 83, 85, 97, 105, 118, 127, 129–131, 142, 161, 162, 165
scale xix, 73, 105, 108, 110, 113, 121, 143, 148, 154, 173, 174
schematic 136
sealer 25, 129, 130
Set-Up xiii, 67, 82, 114, 137, 154, 155
shaping 96, 97
Shop xxvii, 1, 2, 4, 7, 12, 54, 162, 166

slot 32–34, 37, 39, 64, 66, 70–72, 73, 76, 78, 81, 85, 86, 89, 90, 108, 113, 119, 127, 130, 142, 146–148
solvents 125
spacing 145, 149
spray 1, 9, 25, 49, 75, 111, 126, 128, 130, 131, 134
Spruce 31, 108, 173
stain 127–130, 134
string xxvii, xxviii, 5, 37, 63, 105, 106, 117, 135, 137, 141, 142, 145, 145–153, 173
Supplies 7, 157–168

T

Tailpiece 116, 121, 135, 138, 139, 141, 148, 174
tape 8, 49, 61, 72, 75, 85, 105, 115, 116, 118, 119, 127–130, 134, 136
techniques xiii, xviii, xix, xxviii, 26, 51, 89, 114, 132, 135
tension 5
thinning 125
Titebond 11
tone 31, 35, 36, 37, 38, 99, 105, 125, 127, 128, 135, 160, 173, 174

Tools xviii, xxvii, xxviii, 1, 2, 90, 91, 157, 160–168
top ix, x, xviii, 3–5, 9–12, 15–17, 18, 26, 31, 32, 35, 37, 40, 41, 43, 45, 46, 47, 49, 54, 58, 59, 62, 63, 68, 69, 77, 78, 85, 86, 88–92, 97–107, 116–118, 120–122, 126, 129–131, 134, 136, 142–144, 146, 150, 153, 173
top coats 129–131, 134
truss rod ix, 38, 48, 62, 63, 64, 71, 72, 81, 95, 127, 130, 135, 137, 140, 151, 153, 173
type xvii, xviii, 1, 2, 3, 6, 7, 11, 25, 51, 63, 99, 105–107, 135, 136, 138, 141

V

Veneers xviii, 3, 5, 7, 10–12, 26, 157, 158
volume 105, 130, 135, 154

W

water 4, 12, 25, 85, 105, 125, 127, 131, 134
white 25, 86, 88, 114, 140, 150, 173
wood for 5

DESCRIPTION OF ENGLISH GUITARS MODELS

Common Features on all models:
- Custom neck to customer specs
- All available in 7-string models
- TV Jones pickups
- 3 pc. maple neck-ebony center
- Maestro has hand carved spruce top
- Laminated top, back, sides on Model 1, Esquire, Jazz King
- Single cut-away
- Multiple bindings
- Gold or white mother of pearls inlays
- Neck joined at 16th Fret
- 22 carat yellow or white gold leaf under pick guard, truss rod cover and pickup rings
- Nelson tone stabilizer bar
- O-Fret
- Adjustable truss rod
- Ebony fretboard
- English nec-loc system
- Unique 'F' holes match inlays
- All available in plain or flammed maple
- 25" scale-different scales available – also custom colors

Model 1 on Front Cover: #1

- Country orange burst
- 25" scale
- 17" wide
- 3" thick
- Mother of pearl inlaid knobs
- 16:1 Grover imperial tuners
- Bigsby tailpiece
- Schaller rollermatic bridge

Jazz King on Back Cover: #2

- 3 1/4" thick
- 25" scale
- 17" wide
- Fixed tailpiece
- Single pick-up of choice
- Volume & tone control

Maestro on Back Cover: #3

- Hand carved spruce top
- 25" scale
- 3" thick
- 17" wide
- 16:1 Gotoh tuners – ebony buttons
- Ebony tailpiece, pickguard, headstock veneer
- Single Kent Armstrong floating pickup

The Esquire Model is the same as Model 1 only it is 2 5/16" thick

Plaster of Paris
2 Part Epoxy ~~Resin~~ Molding Resin
Release Agent

VENEER [====] MAPLE .040 - .050
[====] MAPLE .030 -
[====] POPLAR .020
[====] MAPLE .030

NET .120

805. L SAN YSIDRO
AFTER 2 Lights
shopping center w/ 99¢ store
KRAGEN # 3-<' - 400.